FOR GOD'S

Donald Reeves was born in Ma
Sherborne School.

He served in the Royal Sussex Regiment, 1952–54, and then studied at Queens' College, Cambridge. He was a British Council lecturer in Beirut, 1957–60, and tutor at Brasted Theological College, 1960–61. After training at Cuddesdon Theological College, 1960–63, he was ordained in 1963. He has since served churches in Maidstone (1963–65) and Morden (1969–80), and was Chaplain to the Bishop of Southwark (1965–68).

Since 1980 Donald Reeves has been Rector of St James's Church, Piccadilly, where he carries out a unique ministry, both to the many people who work locally and to the thousands of visitors who come to London every year.

FOR GOD'S SAKE

Donald Reeves

Foreword by Monica Furlong

Collins
FOUNT PAPERBACKS

First published in Great Britain
by Fount Paperbacks, London in 1988

Printed and bound in Great Britain by
William Collins Sons & Co. Ltd, Glasgow

CONTENTS

ACKNOWLEDGEMENTS

This book has been written in the midst of a busy life at St James's Church, Piccadilly. I would therefore like to thank publicly my close friends and colleagues who have shown such patience and forbearance during this time. And especially I would like to thank Peter Pelz, who illustrated the cover, for his critical appreciation, and Linda Maude, my secretary, who not only typed and retyped the manuscript but encouraged me in the writing of it.

DONALD REEVES

FOREWORD

At the moment there are any number of voices suggesting what kind of Church we are going to need now. Some favour a clinging to tradition or to fundamentalist interpretations of the Bible; in an uncertain world certainties can be very comforting. Some see churchgoing and the Christian religion as part of the process of becoming upwardly mobile – religion and respectability have ancient intertwining roots that are hard to sever. Some believe that religion is all about sexual morality, keeping people "in order". Some insist that faith is tied inextricably to political action. Others maintain that it is about a "pure" spirituality.

Donald Reeves writes from the heart of one of the most extraordinary churches in the kingdom – St James's, Piccadilly, London, W.1. Lively in liturgy, bold in controversy, concerned about racism, sexism, ecology, art, and much else, under Donald's leadership it has pioneered a new sort of town church and attracted many intelligent women and men who have waited long and patiently for the "new look" in Christianity. Already it shows us preshadowings of a possible way – humane, experimental, unpompous, commonsensical, sensitive, flexible, interesting – a world away from the old rigidities and timidities which bored or lectured whole congregations out of the pews.

Donald himself sees St James's as one of the "centres of good will, of radical compassion" which, with a revived liberalism, will, he believes, form the basis for a new Reformation. Caring for the poor, for people of other races and religions, treating women, homosexuals, and others, with justice, being globally concerned, are never very popular ideas, yet it is such generosity of spirit and absence of prejudice that Donald sees as the blueprint of the coming Christianity. "Liberal is the opposite" he quotes Alec Vidler "not of conservatism but of fanatical or bigoted or intransigent." Donald suggests, I think with truth, that in Church and society there is a worrying movement away from such generosity, and that the question for those of us who are not bigoted or fanatical is how to preserve the quality of spacious human caring that alone releases a redeeming love.

What Donald seems to me to stand for is an effective realism that tries to set aside sentimentality, brutal dogmatism, cruel moralistic attitudes and intolerance, and to see the human lot as clearly as possible – to see it and to do the best that can be done to ameliorate what is intolerable in it. In a time of nuclear and environmental threat, of catastrophic war, of desperate hunger and want, of nationalistic hatred, of fierce ideologies, of fear and contempt for those who are "not like us", it is extraordinarily painful to try to look squarely at the world in which we find ourselves, and it is not easy to remain hopeful when we do so. St James's, through Donald's influence, has resolutely set itself to this task, and the task itself defines what Christian faith must be – retaining genuine hope and joy in the face of agony, apathy, cruelty and despair.

Donald's book describes wherein his hope lies, wherein our hope (as citizens of a world desperately struggling for survival) must lie too. All possible strength to his elbow and good sales to his book.

MONICA FURLONG

PREFACE

Over sixty years ago that great Christian writer and thinker, R. H. Tawney, wrote these prophetic words in his book *The Acquisitive Society*:

> He hath put down the mighty from their seat and hath exalted the humble and meek. A society which is fortunate enough to possess so revolutionary a basis, a society whose founder was executed as the enemy of law and order, need not seek to soften the materialism of principalities and powers with mild doses of piety administered in an apologetic whisper.

Today, as never before in our lifetime, those of us who seek, however feebly, to put those words of Tawney's into practice find the Church and ourselves attacked by those very powers and principalities which Tawney mentions.

Ever since his Falklands Islands sermon in St Paul's Cathedral in 1982, the Archbishop of Canterbury has, in the perceptive words of a leading article in *The Observer*, consistently refused to act as "an echo chamber for the new moral certainties of Thatcherism", and for this he has been subjected to what can only be described as a vicious campaign of destabilization by the most reactionary elements of Church and State, which are in such ascendancy today; aided and abetted by very large sections of our servile and sycophantic Press.

This campaign has now been widened to include all those of us who seek to cherish and protect liberal values, liberal in their broadest non-party sense – liberal in generosity of spirit, liberal in nobility of heart and mind, liberal in tolerance, liberal in a care for our ethnic minorities, for women, for gay people, all unpopular causes and classes in today's harsh and illiberal world.

And since these unfavourable times and circumstances seem destined to continue for some considerable period, it is vitally

11

important that there should be centres of good will, of radical compassion, of those very liberal values for which we must work – for that new Reformation which we so desperately need, and for which purpose this book has been written.

It has therefore been dedicated to Archbishop Trevor Huddlestone, CR, to Dr Una Kroll, to Nadir Dinshaw, and to the memory of Bishop John Robinson, who in their very different ways incarnate in themselves these values, and to whom many people both inside the Church of England and outside it, owe a great debt of gratitude.

INTRODUCTION

In the centre of a tiny Cotswold village, there is a small twelfth-century church. The church clock stopped many years ago at two thirty. The graveyard is unkempt, and it is not easy to find a path to the entrance. The church is locked all the time, except when services are held once every two weeks; a handful of elderly people gather for worship, led by a priest who has four other churches under his care, and who in his heart wonders what he is doing.

Round about the church, cottages of mellow Cotswold stone are being imaginatively extended and lovingly restored. Their owners are either weekenders or energetic commuters from Birmingham or London.

There are rumours that the church will be declared redundant, and then sold as "an unusual residential property, requiring alteration, standing in its own ground".

No one bothers about the church building. The little congregations are too frail, and do not know what to do. The new residents have other priorities – recovering after their hectic working weeks, and making their own homes as comfortable and their gardens as colourful as possible. Meanwhile, the House of God stands derelict and nearly abandoned.

On warm, still, sunlit summer evenings, that village scene looks idyllic. Yet it haunts me. I am dismayed by the abandoned church, which after eight hundred years is a poignant sign of the collapse of English Christianity. Although the church is in the centre of the village, its activities are irrelevant to the lives of almost everybody there.[1]

This book attempts to map out the contours of a Reformation whereby the Christian religion can have a wholesome part to play in the life of our society. I am not presenting a blueprint; the outlook for the future of the world is so uncertain that it is foolish to forecast the shape and character of organized religion.

What I have tried to do is to map out the contours of a new Reformation. They are indistinct. Many details have to be filled in, but the contours are an indispensable guide to getting the debate going about the identity and nature of Christianity in the foreseeable future.

It is not usually noted what a battering the Christian religion has taken in the last two hundred years, so that today there is little confidence left in religious institutions. There has been the gradual process of secularization whereby society freed itself from religion, and discovered its own autonomy.[2] How and when this process happened is still a matter for careful enquiry, but certainly up to and by 1914 the influence of religion had been considerably eroded. Theories of scientific materialism, and the scientific method of analysis of explanation, had come to be seen as entirely adequate as a way of describing human experience.

And then from 1914 onwards, we have experienced and are aware of an unprecedented accumulation of human tragedy, brought about sometimes by the inevitable consequences of modern war, and sometimes by sheer human wickedness. Events like Hiroshima and the Holocaust defy easy explanation. They numb the senses and deaden the imagination.

Thus, it is not easy to speak about God. God has been expelled and has disappeared. God appears to be a spent force powerless to intervene. For the majority of people in Britain, God is neither here nor there; and for some years theologians have spoken of the eclipse of God, the absence of God, the darkness of God – even the death of God.

Christianity has survived – but only just. It has done so by retreating and caving in. Vigorous as it is in suburbia, Christianity has been well and truly privatized. Christian belief and practice have been reduced and domesticated to the life of the soul, the home and the family. Such religion offers consolation, but it is not expected to venture beyond the church door. In this way, Christianity has avoided confrontation with the turbulence, confusions and disturbances of our age. As a hobby, churchgoing for the few fits easily into our bleak landscape. But interaction with anything else is regarded with suspicion. The clergy – especially bishops – are urged to give a moral lead (as long as this "lead" is restricted to matters of sexual morality), but in the eyes of the public, they are expected to keep quiet about everything else.

But the retreat of Christianity before this sense of the absence of God has more sinister aspects. There are, for example, those who unwittingly endorse the fatalism and hopelessness. They peddle a bastard form of Christianity; they are found in all denominations, among bishops, clergy and laity. These are the people who say we live in a fallen world, that human beings are depraved and that we are not set on this earth to be happy. Original sin is the only doctrine they seem to know about. They believe we need tough government to prevent us from destroying each other. The world is a Vale of Tears; this life is just a preparation for God's judgement as to whether we shall end in heaven or hell. Any energy left over is to be used in helping others, but no one should expect to make much difference. Such a religion is Conservative in practice and in politics. The job of the clergy, they say, is to teach people to pray, read the Bible and attend church with the aim of saving souls. Those who advocate such an understanding of religion are invariably well-to-do, financially secure and enjoy religion as an "extra". They resent what they call the political clergy – from the inner cities (who are usually much poorer than they).

These fatalists are joined by others who are on an indulgent trip down memory lane. Nostalgia is their password. They are "religious revivalists" favouring a return to a sterner Way, Truth and Life. They object to the Archbishop of Canterbury, who they say is lacking in principles, authority, charisma and proper dedication to the Church of England. They resent the concern of the Church for the World, and prefer established paternalism – the restoring of almshouses to the poor. They believe the Church should teach and preach the ancient Word of God rather than accommodate the Gospel to the world. They are for the Prayer Book and against the Alternative Service Book. They dislike women priests. They disapprove of the Church's "wet" attitude in agreeing to marry divorced people. They consider the way our ancient buildings are used to be irresponsible. They think the Church is short on sin and heavy on mateyness. They write elegantly and trenchantly. These are the expressions of a sizeable population of conservative Christians who feel that the Church has betrayed them in flirting with modern trends. They conjure up a past which never existed, and are unashamedly nostalgic for the days of Biggles and Enid Blyton, stretching back to Merry Old England. But nostalgia destroys hope. It is one of the enemies of true religion, because it prevents truth from getting a look in; it fosters illusions. After all, looking back is the best way to avoid looking at what is happening now. Such people join the cynics and fatalists who believe that nothing can be done.

The last group which has to be mentioned here, the Fundamentalists, are the most pernicious. Their religion is based on slogans – "the Bible says", "Jesus says", "the essence of Christianity is" . . . They are a rapidly growing sect within Christianity, particularly among young people. They sense the uncertainty of the age, so they offer clean, dogmatic answers to every question. They provide security and safety for their followers (thus aping many of the cults they themselves condemn). Their arrogance and absurd claims that the Bible is free of error, their anti-intellectualism, their cruel moralistic attitudes, their intolerance of other Christians and members of other faiths, need to be constantly exposed and attacked by the mainstream churches. They have hope for the world to come, but little or none for the world we actually live in.[3]

Cynics, reactionaries, sentimentalists, fundamentalists, and all those who expect nothing more from the practice of their religion than a little folksy cheering up turn away from the bitter chill outside, and busy themselves with their own personal concerns. Their narcissism, taking delight and pleasure in themselves, is not just a sign of immaturity, but is repugnant to any understanding of Christian faith which is directed towards the other, the broken, the wounded, the dispossessed and the poor.

The avoidance of pain, and resistance to seeing what is there, just allow everything to get worse and worse. They may justify themselves by their religious activities, they may deceive themselves that they are doing their duty by the performance of rituals and the activity of their worship. They may even congratulate themselves on the warmth of the community they have created and on the constructive meetings they have. But nothing happens, nothing is changed.

This sort of religion has failed people again and again. It makes people pessimistic, selfish and introspective. It feeds on all sorts of fear – of the unusual, of women, and of the sensual and sexual. It mistrusts the artist, and the divine gift of imagination and creativity. It is invariably reactionary, frequently racist, often anti-Semitic.

The contours of a new Reformation suggest something quite different: that in God's creation, there is much we have to learn from the stirring of God's spirit – in the cries of the poor and the coloured, in the energy and passion among many women, in the inspiration of the artist, in the experience of the mystic, in the glad recognition of the gift of the presence of other religions and other cultures, in the awareness of the pain the earth experiences at our insensitive treatment of it, and in the care among those who bother about it, in placing the Kingdom of God for which Jesus Christ lived and died as central to a renewed vision, and by celebrating the affirming our Jewish roots.

In these stirrings and promptings of the human heart, God is no longer distant or absent, but very close. A Reformation begins with the awareness of the closeness of God in all these struggles and aspirations.[2] Without a willingness to listen to these movements of the human spirit, there will be no Reformation. The poor, the artist and poet, women, the Jew, the Buddhist, Hindu or Muslim – the teachings and life of Jesus Christ – and the experience of two thousand years of Christianity, where it is attended to with seriousness – all these diverse and disparate experiences become our teachers. Reformation starts when the churches throw aside the siege mentality which has overtaken us all, and move out in faith to the open country.

Reformation cannot be managed. It will not appear on the agenda of councils and synods; and Reformation is not popular, particularly among churches and church leaders. No one likes to be disturbed (I have myself been disturbed by some of what I have written!), especially those who hold the power, and are paid by the institution. Squabbles about the ordination of women and between liberals and traditionalists are mild compared to what could be if we were open to these movements of the human spirit and to God's Spirit. And the best way to begin is to return to the roots and source of faith, and that means attention to the religion of the Jewish people, and the ministry of Jesus.

1

Jesus for Justice

In Auschwitz there was a group of learned Jews, including some rabbis. On Sunday afternoons they were left undisturbed, and one afternoon, out of fear, anger and despair, they decided to put God on trial. The case for the prosecution was overwhelming; the case having been made, the "judges" had no difficulty in reaching their verdict. God was found guilty of neglecting His chosen people. The sentence was passed, silence fell upon the assembly. Then an elderly, frail rabbi stood up. "Nevertheless," he said, "let us not forget, it is time for our evening prayers."[1]

That story, and the diaries, prayers and paintings of the Jews in the death camps, witness to the heroic endurance, persistence and courage of the Jewish people, who, as they ignored their God, cursed and denied their God, yet still spoke of Him. The Jews recorded their experience for the sake of the future, even though the world was not listening and did not care. They wrote ceaselessly. They could not keep silent. Far from being a symbol of hopelessness, the witnesses of the Holocaust experienced it as a warning, a summons to renewal in religious faith and a challenge for us all to seek ways of living in peace and justice, even amid the unbearable fear, terror and dread of the death camps. If there is meaning in the Holocaust, it has to be gleaned from that witness. Metaphysical explanations which are above it or beyond it are blasphemous.

The Christian system, offering answers to the questions of life, disintegrates before the experience of the Holocaust,[2] and cannot after a few years be dusted down, tidied up and brought out once again. There is something offensive in the way Christian writers have recently begun to appropriate the Holocaust experience for themselves; they often use the following story, for the echoes of the Crucifixion are obvious.

19

An execution was to take place. The camp commander refused to serve as hangman. Three SS men took over the job. Three necks were placed into three nooses within a short moment. "Long live freedom!", shouted the grown-ups. But the child, the third person on the scaffold, said nothing. "Where is God now? Where is He?" said someone behind me. The three chairs had tipped over. We marched past. The two men were no longer alive – but the third body, the child's, was still twitching; the child was lighter, and therefore still living. Behind me I heard the same man ask, "Where is God now?" And behind me I heard an answering voice, "Where is He? Here He is – he hangs on the gallows." That night, the soup tasted of corpses.[2]

That story belongs to the Jewish people. It is their story, not ours, since it was Christians who either sent the Jews to their deaths, or turned a blind eye, or left them in hell, "where God and humankind, full of horror, look into each other's eyes".[3]

Christians have not only to acknowledge their collusion, wrongdoing and guilt, and ask the Jews for forgiveness. They have also to attend to these formidable witnesses of the fortitude and courage of the human spirit.

That witness on the part of the Jews was not called out of a few courageous individuals. For thousands of years it had been part of the genius of the people who believed that God was with them; that God was not capricious (like all the other gods around them), but continually, consistently and for ever faithful to the people He had chosen, whatever they might do as perpetrators or victims of injustice. Even as Abraham was quarrelling with God, as Moses was talking with God, Jacob wrestling with God; even as God felt betrayed by the infidelity of His people; even as the prophets cursed God for the uncomfortable job he had given them to do, there nevertheless abides the sense that God would never abandon His people. Amidst all the fatalism and the suffering, the lack of faith and the pride and arrogance of the Jewish people, there is this conviction that God, the power of the good, goodness itself, has the last word. All God required was that His people should live justly and in peace; then they would know God. The metaphor of covenant and partnership is a way of describing the Jewish people's sense of calling and destiny, this special relationship which in its apparent superiority has angered and irritated Gentiles over the centuries.

But the Christian religion was born on Jewish soil. In spite of the strains of anti-Semitism in the gospels (reflecting the early quarrels between Christians and Jews), the Jewishness of Christianity has to be remembered and recalled if Christianity in our own day is to have any meaning. Jesus was a Jew; he was dark skinned and spoke Aramaic. He lived out of the familiar conviction that God was with him – in the way his people had done for centuries and have done up to today, as we have seen. Christianity is an Eastern religion. The Old Testament is the Jewish Bible, and, for the formative part of the growth and development of Christianity, the only Bible. The Christian God is the Jewish God.

Jesus reveals God. That is why I have to write about him, and add a few more to the millions of words already written. I find a lot of indifference about the person of Jesus. He is such a familiar name, yet the familiarity conceals astonishing ignorance about him. This ignorant familiarity is caused by the way the churches have tamed and diminished Jesus: since he does not belong to this world, he does not much matter. London Weekend Television undertook a poll on the person of Jesus Christ. It showed that Jesus was regarded as God dressed up as a man. To prove he was God he walked on water, performed miracles frequently and effortlessly, and was untouched by pain. His death on the Cross was God's way of offering forgiveness for our sins.

That nicely disposes of Jesus. He does not make any difference to our lives today; such a Jesus is just not interesting. Ask around about the nature of God, particularly among those who are bothered about a religious or spiritual dimension, and rarely is that connection made with Jesus. God is like – well, God is in everything, God is everywhere, God is out there, God is a cosmic blur. God is like a policeman, a judge, a stern father. God is weary and grumpy having to listen to all our requests – or so

He is depicted in Mel Calman's cartoons. God is universal love. The experience of God is like diving into a pile of old clothes – comforting and slightly musty. God is like an inner voice; God is the voice of creation. God is the supreme artist. God is hanging around like a gooseberry. God is so private and close that He is like a personal possession, like a clean handkerchief or spare set of keys.

But the Christian tradition says quite simply and directly that God is as God is in Jesus. Look at Jesus, and there is God.

We have to put aside the popular preconceptions about Jesus, for we have used and abused Jesus for our own ends. We have to peel away all the prejudices, opinions and ideas and let his words speak to us as directly as possible. The New Testament was written in the light of the conviction that Jesus was Messiah, Lord and Saviour: indeed, there are over two hundred ways in which, on reflection of the extraordinary impact Jesus had on those first Christians, the Risen Jesus is described. As the Christian movement turned into a fully developed major religion, complete with its own mythology of Creation, Paradise, Disobedience and Fall, Redemption and Salvation, so the imagination of St Paul and many others was extended to its limits to describe the power of this Messiah raised from the dead, present among them in His spirit.

The gospels too reflect this perception of Jesus; they were written after the Resurrection for propaganda, teaching and encouragement in anticipation that the world was coming to an end. Nevertheless, through the rays of the light of the exalted Christ, it is possible to listen to the words of Jesus and to attend to what he did as a man of his time rather than as the object of Christian faith.

Jesus's message was that the kingdom of God was at hand. He did not speak about God directly. He did not start an organization. He was reticent about himself – he accepted no title and he claimed none. His concern was for the Kingdom of God.[4] He was like a Jewish prophet, except that he spoke directly on his own authority (whereas the prophets said, "Thus saith the Lord"). He was a teacher, an exorcist and a healer. He sprang from the Jewish soil as one who had dug deep into the depths of Judaism, and emerged with a sort of Jewishness refined and transformed – recognizably Jewish but something more. He was fearless in his teaching, and where necessary questioned all tradition. He was a man of formidable independence and courage. His clarity in looking into the basic motives of human behaviour was such that, confronted by it, the listener seemed to be naked before God. He spoke the truth. He scandalized the powerful and the wealthy. He had an appalling reputation among his family and in his town of Nazareth, because he plainly enjoyed himself eating and drinking with the poor. There is very little internal evidence of what he felt about his mission; but from the intimate way he addressed God – as "Abba" or Daddy – he was in a remarkable and unparalleled way living out the familiar Jewish conviction that God was with him. Just occasionally, the curtain is raised and there is a glimpse of the centre of Jesus, as in St Luke, chapter 10 verse 1, when Jesus sends out the disciples in pairs for their mission. On their return, they tell him that they had been able to expel evil demons. Jesus cried out, exalted, vibrant and triumphant, as one conscious of taking part in a struggle of cosmic dimensions and confident in God's ultimate victory: "I beheld Satan as lightning fall from heaven. Behold, I give unto you power to tread on serpents and scorpions and over all the power of the enemy; and nothing shall by any means hurt you" (Luke 10:18–19).

There is no systematic teaching about the Kingdom. Jesus speaks in riddles, tells disturbing stories, reveals the absurdity of men (so that when he announces that God is near ... people excuse themselves – one's got to go to his father's funeral; another says he has to go home to say goodbye to everyone (Luke 10:59–62). His teaching is oblique and indirect. He occasionally preaches in synagogues, but his work is done on the move. He gathers a tiny band of followers – most of whom do not understand what he is up to – and he is always travelling, as if to avoid those who were out to get him. So the lake and the shore, the hills and the desert are favoured haunts.

His message is addressed to the Galilean peasants. He offers good news to the poor, to all those who are dependent on the charity of others and thus feel humiliated – the sick and disabled, the blind and the crippled, the dumb and the deaf; to those who were despised by society – the prostitutes and thieves, the tax collectors (they were regarded as dishonest), and all those who could not read or write (and so failed to observe the complicated laws of the Jewish religion, because they could not understand them); to the widows and orphans – dependent on charity; to those who had little or no work. In other words, the Gospel was offered to the excluded, the dispossessed, the despised and downtrodden. When he ate with them or healed them, they knew he was a man from God, and all their shame and disgrace were wiped out.

The poor longed for a Messiah. The idea of the Kingdom of God had been present in Jewish history from the setting up of the monarchy under King David a thousand years before Christ, to the longing for the establishment of God's Kingdom in Jesus's day. Palestine was a major centre for revolt against the Roman Empire, and the Jews hoped for a time when a mighty, military Messiah would emerge and destroy the Romans. The Kingdom is not therefore primarily an "idea", but the way in which men and women live together before God.

In the announcement of the Kingdom, Jesus declared its arrival. At the heart of it is Jesus's compassion. Today compassion often means taking pity on someone a bit less fortunate than we are ourselves; it means handing over a few crumbs, and carries with it a sense of superiority and patronage. There are no English words which do justice to the Greek word for compassion used in the gospel. It is a much stronger sense of the phrase "moved to do this or that"; it is what is experienced in the guts at the sight of pain or anguish, of the humiliation, the shame and the disgrace of the poor and unwanted. Jesus placed himself with the poor; that was why as a middle-class rabbi he chose to live with them.

Henri Nouwen, in his book *Compassion*, tells of a doctor in a Central American country who has worked among the poor for too many years. His patients come on foot or on horseback, and tell him their troubles. The doctor recognizes how the peasants are being exploited, and becomes one of their spokesmen. The government needs to shut him up, so they torture and kill his 17-year-old son. Instead of dressing his body in finery for the funeral, the doctor and his wife decide to leave the burnt and mangled body on the blood-stained bed, so that the community can see the full extent of the evil that has been perpetrated. The doctor is also an artist; for years he had sketched the people – expressing the endurance, the courage and the patience of the people he regarded it as a privilege to live and work among. After his son's death, through his tears and exhaustion, he goes on drawing and sketching, determined that the world should know the extent of this injustice.

The doctor's compassion finds echoes in the ministry of Jesus. Jesus's healings and exorcisms, his forgiveness and the way he kept company with the poor, removed their humiliation and their guilt. They knew they had God's approval. The faith of Jesus, which was so contagious, was simply faith that the goodness and power of God was stronger than all the fatalism and powerlessness that was so prevalent.

The Sermon on the Mount describes his ministry's priorities. The Sermon is not much concerned with religious matters, but with matters such as money, possessions, power, anxiety, sexuality, how to treat neighbours and enemies; these are matters on which everyone has to decide. The Beatitudes are the core of the Sermon. A blessing is a mysterious action: it is that which confers or conveys life. Those who are blessed are the poor both in substance and in spirit, for they need God; those who weep for the world will receive comfort. The meek and the gentle are promised the earth for their reward. Those who love justice and show mercy – to them will be shown mercy. The pure in heart will see God. The peacemakers are blessed, and those who suffer unjustly are also blessed. Jesus urges those who wish to live in the Kingdom to live simply, and trust that God will provide everything. We are to turn the other cheek, and to love our enemies. To live in this way we shall then be like salt and light. Everything we need will be given. We shall be known and judged by the fruit we bear – that is, by what we do.

The Sermon on the Mount reverses all normal values; it is neither reasonable nor respectable. Much of it seems absurd – it is so idealistic, so foolish as to be impossible. Yet it deserves careful and close scrutiny, because the effect of allowing the words to sink in can be to experience a sense of return, of coming home. There is a sanity about it which contrasts strongly with the values of our own crazy and lost world. The offer of God's goodness is ultimately shown and revealed, when nothing gets in the way of receiving and acknowledging it – hence the privileged place for the powerless and the weak and all those who are prepared to be vulnerable to the presence of pain and suffering.

Jesus invited men and women to enter the Kingdom. This conversion is not, however, just a private, personal experience; it involves a turning from the allegiance of the "world" – from selfishness, ambition, the search for power and prestige, from all those values which promote injustice – towards the priorities of the Kingdom. To enter the Kingdom and to accept the invitation is to experience a warming of the heart in acknowledging the goodness of God; but no part of living is untouched.

It is easy, through a sense of ill-informed familiarity, to miss the disturbing, absolute nature of Jesus's message. Those who would become his followers were required to leave their families, their trade, and to be prepared for a life of daily uprootedness and insecurity. They had to be ready for ridicule, persecution, even death. Their commitment had to be complete and unconditional; and if they were to hold special positions in the community, they were required to feel and behave as if they were slaves or children; they were to refuse all titles and privileges.

Jesus required those with possessions to share them with the poor. There was no place for hoarders in God's Kingdom. Wealth was seen as an obstacle to salvation: it was false treasure, offering false security and a constant source of anxiety.

Jesus's message is radical. It is rigorous, demanding, impossible and Utopian. In the history of Christianity, these radical requirements have either been watered down, ignored or adopted by a special group of people, thus relieving everyone else of their responsibilities. (In the second century, for example, some Christians were required to take the vow of celibacy in some Syrian churches before Baptism; and there are many examples in history of Christian communities trying to live out simply the vision of the Kingdom.)

But there is something elusive about Jesus's teaching about the Kingdom. Certainly wherever the values of the Kingdom prevail then there is the Kingdom. Conversely, where those values are denied there is, in New Testament terms, the Kingdom of Satan. But God's Kingdom is not identical with some Utopian socialist state. In the gospels, the Kingdom is both present and near at hand; that means that it is always unfinished and incomplete. The love and justice of God's Kingdom will never ever be realized this side of the grave. Kingdom Christians have a strong sense of the possibilities which the future offers, as if God were eternally young.

At Jesus's death, the message of the Kingdom of God disappeared. It had, from an historical perspective, failed. As the Christian religion grew out of the Jesus movement, so the Kingdom of God was diminished and changed. Jesus's teaching had been to the poor of Galilee; it was a primitive, Aramaic-speaking community; the Christian religion now addressed a predominantly mixed, urban and Greek-speaking community in the Roman Empire.

Thus, whereas Jesus's message offered hope and dignity to the poor in this life, Paul addresses all individuals as needing salvation, without distinguishing between rich and poor. As Christianity spread its influence, and became the established religion of the Roman Empire, the subversive Kingdom of Jesus was changed. Entry into the Kingdom was reduced to a state of inner transformation, leaving the external world untouched, or, alternatively, such entry was postponed until after death. Either way, the comfortable and the rich preferred a state of affairs which would not alter their material circumstances, and since most theologians and scholars lived privileged lives, they too inevitably reduced or diminished the centrality of Jesus's message about the Kingdom.

But this is no longer so. On the one hand, more and more scholars are trying to place Jesus in history, in his time; and on the other, among Christians, mostly in the Third World, there is an expression of longing and hope to return to the sanity of the values and priorities of the Kingdom. In El Salvador and Nicaragua, in Brazil, in South Africa – even fitfully and quietly in Europe – there are emerging Christian communities whose identity is shaped by their loyalty to the Kingdom of God in their struggle for liberation and justice, and in their quest to recover the fundamental communion which exists between all men and women and creation and God. Jesus's announcement of the Kingdom in what he said and did, and asked of those who followed him, was, in effect, to show the tender and gracious face of God; the radical demands he made were the working out of the commandment, "You will love your God with all your heart . . . and your neighbour as yourself."

Christians speak of Jesus as Lord, in families, congregations, all sorts of groups and churches holding the Utopian vision of the Kingdom before them; this means that such communities will always be disturbing, troubled, untidy, and never completely at home with the radical message because there is no way of measuring it. It is a Utopia that does not drain energies, but gives fuller life; it is a vision which, if taken seriously, creates a tension without which churches stagnate and die. It is a vision which is not just about inner attitudes, but about the whole of life – politics and economics, the work that we do, the way power is exercised; and the way relationships are handled. There is no special, spiritual realm. Everything and everyone can be part of the flow of giving birth to God's Kingdom.

In his humanity, Jesus reveals God. Christianity is not concerned with ghosts or haloes and auras of holiness. If we think of God as remote and powerful, Jesus on the contrary reveals one who no longer distances himself from those who most fear him, but is with them to serve them; Jesus relinquishes all power and on the Cross becomes a victim. If we think of God as impassive, Jesus reveals a God who is vulnerable and suffers with us. It is an upside-down God we are asked to believe in.

In other words, the nature of God is revealed in that which is must human. How else could it be? How else could you or I or anyone else recognize the love of God? The transcendence of God is manifested in the heart and depths and core of Jesus's humanity. Wherever that humanity takes shape today, there is something God-given, and the release of goodness, love and compassion which then takes place is a sign, a glimpse of God's Kingdom to confound the cynics, reactionaries and fundamentalists.

2

A New Reformation

Fortunately, the coming into being of the Kingdom of God does not depend on the Church. God's grace and initiative are not so restricted. The establishing of God's Kingdom is nothing less than the transformation of all creation – of all that we know of the universe, and of the very much more we do not yet know. When every person and group, all economic and political activity, all artistic inspiration, everything that can be touched, heard or smelt, all of the natural and animal world, reflect and radiate without blemish the goodness and love of God, then the Kingdom will be present in all its diversity and splendour.

Such a vision of the new heaven and earth is found in the Book of Revelation. Much of this bizarre and most neglected book is the story of God's judgement on and punishment of a world and a Roman Empire corrupted by man's arrogance and pride. But all through the book there are intimations of another dimension – of God's ultimate goodness and mercy (the protection of the saints, the wedding feast of the Lamb and his bride); now at last the cries of the martyrs are answered:

> Then I saw a new heaven and a new earth, for the first heaven and the first earth had vanished, and there was no longer any sea. I saw the holy city, new Jerusalem, coming down out of the heaven from God, made ready like a bride adorned for her husband. I heard a loud voice proclaiming from the throne: "Now at last God has his dwelling among men! He will dwell among them and they shall be his people, and God himself will be with them. He will wipe every tear from their eyes; there shall be an end to death, and to mourning and crying and pain; for the old order has passed away!"
>
> Revelation 21:1–4 (New English Bible)

Yet again, the Jewish sense of the goodness of God, of God's presence in creation, is the key to this vision: it is a guiding vision which removes the despair from death; it opens up new horizons. The vision is Utopian, pointing to a future world, and to the end of history when all is gathered into God.

But the future is already present in those tiny glimpses of the Kingdom where strangers become friends, quarrels are patched up, the hungry are fed, the sick are visited and wounds carefully and lovingly tended, where poverty is removed, where the weak discover their strength and the strong their weakness, and where the master/servant relationship is banished. These are signs of the Kingdom of God already present. At the front of Patrick White's novel *The Solid Mandala*, the author introduces these words from Paul Eluard:

There is another world, but it is in this one.

The church is the agent of this Kingdom; without the Church and the story of Jesus and the Kingdom which it retells and celebrates, it would not be possible to recognize even these glimpses of the Kingdom. As an agent, the Church should reflect the priorities and values of the Kingdom. If the allegiances of its members are indifferent or opposed to those of the Kingdom, then the Church gets in the way of belief in the goodness of God; it is a barrier to perceiving what the Kingdom of God is like. In this case the Church itself contributes to that persistent sense of the absence and darkness of God.

And that is the trouble today. Sunday by Sunday the Scriptures are read to us, but, at least as far as the Church of England is concerned, what a lamentable, tribal and limited religion we both profess and practise – far removed from the demands and promises of those who are invited to enter God's Kingdom. Our services and synods, our attitudes and our theology reflect just what we are: white, English, middle-aged and middle-class. Such is the God we reflect, far from the God of the Kingdom of God as disclosed in Jesus. We have made a God in our own image. Our tribal sense of our identity expresses itself in arrogance and condescension to those who do not fit, because it is a feature of our tribal religion that we define everyone else in relation to ourselves.

Look at the implicit racism of the Church of England.

Anglicans present a kindly, liberal aspect: of course, everyone is welcome! The reality, however, is different. Black Anglicans are practically invisible. The mass immigration of the Afro-Carib-bean people after 1947, many of them Anglicans, heralded the beginning of a multi-racial society, but it was ignored by the Church. Black Anglicans play no significant part in the struc-tures of the Church of England. They are absent on public Church/State occasions. Finding themselves unwelcome, they join Pentecostal churches, which rightly and readily nurture African cultural beliefs and practices. And if the black commu-nity has been effectively excluded from the Church of England, the same can be said of working-class men and women, homo-sexuals and the missing generation of young people. However hazy a view we might have of religious institutions, it is not right that they should be exclusive clubs for the moderately well off; and certainly any church which ignores or denies the thrust of the priorities of the Kingdom of God forfeits any claim to be an agent of that Kingdom.

Inevitably, churches which flourish in suburbia reflect subur-ban values; if they did not, they would not flourish. Here religion is a matter of private and personal taste; the practice of religion endorses the spirit of competition, following a career, getting on and up in the world. Anything which questions all this is treated with much suspicion.

For those who share the vision of the Kingdom of God, the question is how such a church can become an agent for the Kingdom. If in Jesus's time his message was good news for the poor (and he did not forget the rich, provided they were prepared to share or relinquish their possessions), how can it be so today? The poor have to answer that for themselves, but as things are, there is sufficient evidence of the captivity of the suburban church for any observer to answer that the Gospel is not good news for the poor.

What can be done? How can a middle-class church change its priorities and its allegiance from Churchianity to those of the Kingdom?

Initially, the Church of England has to be prepared to undergo a time of self-criticism – something like a time of corporate repentance. This is not just a call for public humiliation or for washing dirty linen in public. It is much more an opportunity to see what needs to be removed, so that the Church may be purged and purified, for an institution in decline can only either reduce its activities, and do the same things in a more limited way, or thrash around looking for new gimmicks to change the situation.

It is helpful to this process of self-criticism to remember that there is a history of cleansing, purging and purifying, perhaps most notably in the Reformation of the sixteenth century. Today another Reformation will emerge as a result of this cleansing. In England there is a slender, fitful history of those who have stressed the centrality of the Kingdom of God, a history usually ignored, and thus generally unknown. One of its banners was that of Christian Socialism. William Temple, Archbishop of Canterbury (1942–1946), was the best example of this movement. For a short time he was a member of the Labour Party; he was the first person to use the term "the Welfare State", and has been considered one of the most eminent examples of it. In the nineteenth century, there were many priests working in the slum parishes of the East End of London, and elsewhere, who championed different and varying forms of Christian Socialism – Stewart Headlam's "Guild of St Matthew" was founded in 1877 and campaigned for the nationalization of land. Today, among many small Christian Socialist groups, perhaps the most explicit is the Jubilee Group founded in 1974. In the Jubilee pamphlet – "Politics and the Kingdom – The Legacy of the Anglican Left", John Orens writes:

> By social revolution it is important to remember the Anglican Left did not mean merely a change in economic or political arrangements and certainly not the dull uniformity and bureaucratic tyranny which today masquerades as socialism. Maurice [F. D. Maurice, one of the founding fathers of Christian Socialism, and Professor of Moral Theology at King's College, London, in the 1850s] and those who came after him had one goal: the joyful Kingdom of God on earth. For it they sacrificed their careers and

their reputations. To do so required extraordinary faith and vision. For us, tempted as we are to embrace the fashionable despair of our troubled age, that faith and vision is surely their most abiding legacy.

But the remembering and retelling of history is not all. There has to develop heightened awareness of what the practice of Christianity involves. Today very little is asked of those who become Christians or just fall into embracing Christianity. Christians are expected to believe certain things, read their Bibles and say their prayers. They will be expected to join a church, go to services and take part in church activities, and if they are young and energetic, they will soon find their spare time completely occupied. Clergy are quick to exploit such enthusiasm. Sooner or later their lives will be absorbed by Church.[1]

It is likely that the promptings which drew them to Christianity are ignored, their opportunities to develop as persons denied. They have little time or inclination to steep themselves in the rich tradition of two thousand years' worth of teaching and experience. They will probably feel discouraged. Maybe they will feel depressed and unappreciated. They will either give in or give up. If they give up, they will feel cheated and betrayed.

Their initiation as Christians asked nothing of them beyond the Church; how their Christian faith connected with anything going on in the world outside was tendentious, chancy and vague.

But for those who want to put themselves at the service of the Kingdom, it is a different story. A disciple is someone who binds himself to the master. In the Book of Revelation, struggling, fragile Christian communities under threat of persecution were urged to "follow the Lamb" wherever he went. Here Jesus is seen as the sacrificial victim, which meant that his followers might be called to martyrdom; they had to be prepared, if necessary, to die.

Discipleship has that quality of being bound to one who is inviting a response. It means, in practical terms, a response to the invitation of Jesus to enter the Kingdom. It is therefore right to outline some of the steps – a modern Pilgrim's Progress – for those to whom the Kingdom priorities matter.

Initially what may draw a person to a religious, and then a Christian, belief is personal need. There may well be indifference and lack of any concern about what is happening in the world. Churches inevitably attract many who need encouragement and support just to help them survive.

The next stage is the desire to serve, and to help; somebody wants to do something for another person. But the motives for this helping are often unclear and confused. A housing estate was surrounded by wealthy middle-class suburbs, and each Christmas members of the local rich churches would descend on the estate, laden with food for the poor and elderly. Some of the elderly were wise, and recognized that it was not so much the needs of the poor which were being met (no one ever enquired whether one woman, whom I knew, actually liked tinned apricots, which she was given year after year), as the needs of those who were doing good; their offer of help was well intentioned but not thought out.

For many, this is the final stage of the journey, for the most difficult part is yet to come; and few of us want to embark on it. Helder Camara, a bishop of one of the poorest areas in Brazil, once said, "When I give food to the poor they call me a saint: when I ask why the poor have no food they call me a Communist." To ask "Why?" is threatening, but necessary. It does happen, and when it does it alters the perceptions and even the lives of those who address such questions seriously.

This was brought home to me at St James's, Piccadilly, after the publication of a report called *No Room*, a report commissioned to investigate the problems which surface at night in central London. For six months a worker observed life on the streets, listened to the stories of people he met there, and visited every sort of agency. He presented the report as a sermon. Amongst his recommendations was the establishment of an all-night café for young people. Fifty people responded to this report – they wanted to do something to help. Much enthusiasm was generated.

Some members of the group of fifty were expert in various

fields of work. There was a social worker who knew central London inside out. There was a thoughtful volunteer worker from an Advice Centre who knew many young people; he knew the snags and all the difficulties. There was a Catholic priest who had worked in central London for twenty years. These experts had an invaluable role in helping the others to focus on particular issues. Among the main group, there was yet another group, small at first but it became increasingly important. This group was astonished at the number of people sleeping out, the number of official homeless, the growing numbers of young people who had nowhere to go, and who always had to be on the move. Why, it asked, is this happening? Some began to look at this question in more depth: they began to question the government's housing policy; they saw the reality of community care for discharged mental patients as little more than their being dumped on the streets and abandoned.

At one level this was political education, and a basic introduction to an anlysis of a particular issue. But these discoveries and conversations took place alongside opportunities for prayer and study of the Bible. The group brought their own questions about justice, wealth and poverty to the Bible rather than just tearing out some neutral truth concealed in it. There were also, amidst the dismay at discovering the extent of the problem, those who wanted to analyse it a little more, those who wanted to "get on with it", and the experts, who had heard it all before. Among all this, there was at times a sense of celebration, because, as the project took shape, so they sensed in their work a resonance with the Kingdom of God portrayed in the gospels.

The last stage of the journey is the most difficult yet, but when reached it seems inevitable. Part of this growing awareness is a sense of our unwitting complicity and collusion. We, ourselves, are part of the cause of the problem we are trying to address. Sometimes this creates a feeling of paralysis and guilt; it is easier to give up than to persevere. At this point, too, a sense of disruption and dislocation is experienced: where do we belong? We are not at home here any more. What is it that we can do to show the full extent of that "compassion" which was the hallmark of the ministry of Jesus?

It is at this point that some distinctions have to be made between career and vocation. Vocation is usually associated with being called to "go into the Church" or, more rarely these days, into one of the caring professions. But in fact it is something which concerns anyone who is burning his boats for the service of the Kingdom. A career-orientated person asks questions: "What shall I do?" The person concerned about his or her vocation asks, "Who am I in relation to the God of the Jewish/Christian tradition revealing Jesus in his announcement about the Kingdom? Where, in other words, are my priorities, values and allegiances to be shaped?"

The shaping of anyone's vocation in a Christian setting must involve a community of friends who know each other intimately, take each other seriously, and trust enough to offer different perspectives on aspirations and dreams. Vocations have at different stages to be negotiated. The working out of anyone's vocation is a corporate matter – quite different from the private worrying about "What to do?"

Vocation differs from the notion of a career because of a recognition that there is no fulfilment for an individual unless part of a communal fulfilment. Martin Luther's words of four hundred and fifty years ago are as good a guide as any: "We serve God, we love God, we serve and love our neighbours in community, through vocation." And invariably the pull of discipleship for the Kingdom is, in terms of social probability, downwards – hence the need to distinguish between vocation and career, which is usually about climbing the ladder. Thomas Merton, after twenty years of Trappist life, writes in the preface to the Japanese edition of *The Seven Storey Mountain*, "My monastery is a place in which I disappear from the world as an object of interest in order to be everywhere in it by hiddenness and compassion." The point of such displacement – a move from a normal, usual place – is to become closer to our own weakness and brokenness, and thus more readily to be in a position to work for the Kingdom, and to recognize our common humanity with the poor, the starving, the smelly, the drug addicted – the list is very familiar.

The purging and cleansing of the Church happens when this

process of moving downwards takes place en masse. History is ennobled by such people. St Francis of Assisi, son of a rich merchant, gave his life to God for the poor. The German pastor, Dietrich Bonhoeffer, left the security of New York to return to Nazi Germany and face prosecution and death. Oscar Romero was appointed Archbishop of Salvador in the expectation that he would be a puppet; he listened to the stories of those who had suffered and been tortured; he learnt how nuns and priests had been murdered. He became a bishop for his people; and was shot. Trevor Huddleston, an upper middle class Englishman, became a monk, and then, after living in South Africa in Sophia Town (near Soweto), alerted the world to the evils of apartheid.

Christian discipleship has always to be worked out together with others, for as well as the upholding of the vision, there has to be the nurture of those who are serving it.

Such is the itinerary for those who want to be Christians for today. It is a demanding but bracing and hopeful journey. Along the way the Church meets to celebrate the story of our Redemption and Liberation; to pray together, and to study both the Scriptures and nearly two thousand years of Christian experience so that the clarity of purpose can be sustained; and above all to encourage one another in the activities and projects for the Kingdom.

3

Inner Reformation

In the fourth century, the Roman Emperor, Constantine, decided, for pragmatic and political purposes, to embrace Christianity. He believed that by turning the Christian Church into an imperial cult, a branch of the civil service, and a state religion, he would prevent the disintegration of the Roman Empire. Christian bishops who had once been in the front line of persecution were now loyal to their new Protector, the Emperor. While Jesus expressed his idea of a leader by washing the feet of the disciples, the bishops began to live in palaces, wear crowns and dress in royal colours. They received stipends from the State. They imitated the life style of the Emperor.

There were some who would have no part in this, and they fled to the deserts of Egypt, where, first under the direction of Anthony, a holy and revered monk, they established a religious "alternative" culture, which sought a pure expression of the Christian life. Most of them were peasants, but there were some scholars, and there were a few rich people. Most were men. They came to be known as the Desert Fathers (there were some Mothers too).[1] They lived alone in remote caves, some for many years. Most had some experience of communal living, for this was no "privatized" Christianity; early Christian monasticism had a strong Utopian flavour about it as its members tried to order and live the ideal Christian society. Monks and nuns have always been misunderstood, and the Desert Fathers are no exception. Gibbon, the historian, described them as "hideous, distorted and emaciated beings, without knowledge, without patriotism, without affection, spending their lives in a long routine of useless and atrocious tortures, and quaking before the ghostly phantom of their delirious brains."

But the thrust of the movement was, in spite of some fanaticism, plain: it was to preserve the purity of the Christian

Gospel, to live the Christian life to perfection, and thus to achieve union with God.

In the ancient world, it was believed that the desert was the place where evil spirits and demons lived. When the first monks began to live in remote caves and ravines in order to devote their lives to prayer, they saw themselves as standing in the front line engaged in battle with the Satanic powers.

However remote such interpretations seem to us, they convey unmistakenly a sense of the decisive nature of this spiritual journey, and of the upheaval that accompanies it; for the time of solitude and silence expressed in an extended period of prayer was an occasion where that fundamental trust and reliance in the goodness of God was tested, refined, strengthened and purified.

Now, nearly two thousand years later, those conditions are still absolutely essential for anyone who desires to move beyond the formalities of religious observance; solitude and silence are not easy to come by. Neither are they easy to turn to best advantage. Prayer is a highly problematic activity, for if it is undertaken seriously it can lead initially to a collapse and disappearance of religious belief.

I can best illustrate this personally. My sense of being called to be a priest and my conversion to Christianity virtually coincided. I was enthusiastic about the spiritual life. I began to accumulate a library of books on how to pray and what to do; how to deal with distracting thoughts, how to pray for others. I drew up long lists of people for whom I would regularly pray. There were times when I felt pleased with myself, and then I remembered that pride was the first sin, so I would try to pray more, deny myself food, sleep or sex. When, as invariably happened, I gave in to what seemed to be temptation, I felt guilt and shame, a sense of God's judgement. Either way, my attempts at Christian living were making me more and more miserable. (I realized many years later that this self-disgust and rejection of the world was caused by the misplaced belief that men and women are fundamentally corrupt.)

I persevered. But I began to dread the time I had once given so happily to prayer. It seemed like a one-way conversation; I stopped using words. I read more books about how to use silence and how to meditate. And then, over a period of months, I felt that the God whom I had sought so fervently and who called me to be a priest, had abandoned me. Everything I had joyfully believed in fell away; there were periods of intense boredom. Nothing delighted me any more. Sometimes I felt engulfed by a darkness from which I longed to escape. My job as a curate, and then as a Bishop's chaplain, began to suffer – attending services, preaching and speaking about the Christian faith – and having anything to do with the Church at all became a dreadful burden. It was like a permanent nightmare. I did everything I could to run away from this sense of overwhelming darkness and the fears it brings. (Little did I realize then that everything that grows needs periods of darkness.)

At some point, I made a decision – though how consciously or not I cannot now remember. It was whether to hold on to what little was left of certainty, or just to let go and trust that the darkness and nothingness was not all. There had to be a sort of dying – and only the language of prayer and poetry convey that state. It is like drowning. Water is a recurrent image in the literature on prayer, and the power of that image lies in its danger; the traveller has to be prepared to drown. (This is the fundamental meaning of baptism – the dying of an old life; the burial in the sea is a preparation for the birth of the new person.)

Some will describe what I experienced as just a depression, that could have been cured by suitable medication. Others would have recommended a dose of psychotherapy, where bad childhood memories could be healed. But both medical and psychological categories reduce the experience – only the language of religion, of the mystic, of the poet will do.

It certainly requires courage to experience this sort of stripping, and to stay in such desert places. But provided there are those who can help a traveller befriend, accept and absorb them in all their negativity, then if the experience of those who have been there before us is anything to go by, something new is waiting to be born.

Thomas Merton, the writer and Trappist monk, wrote to his friend, Dorothy Day, on 18th August 1967:

The hermit life is no joke at all – but in it one gradually comes face to face with the awful need of self-emptying, and even of a kind of annihilation so that God may be all, and also the apparent impossibility of it. And of course the total folly of trying to find ways of doing it oneself. The great comfort is in the goodness and sweetness and nearness of all God has made, and the created "isness" which makes Him first of all present in us, speaking to us.

For Thomas Merton it was the "great comfort" that God was there with him in his darkness and in the nothingness he experienced.[2] It was that same sense of God with us that we have noted in the accounts of some of the survivors of the Holocaust, and supremely in the life of Jesus.

It is easy to recognize those who have undertaken this journey into these desert places and then returned. They are people who have a sense of the precious and priceless value of nature, and a joy and delight in it. They laugh readily, particularly at the pretensions of religion. They are uncluttered in their manner, transparent in their love for God and for others.

They also show the compassion of Jesus: their own journey has led them to shed all the illusions they had about themselves, so that they begin to be led into an awareness of the presence of evil and of the suffering and afflictions of their sisters and brothers, and of the pain of the earth itself. The knowledge and peace of God they had, with such cost, discovered at the centre of their being does not lead to a closed communion with God – but to an intense experience of intercommunion, interdependence, interconnectedness with all Creation, and a recognition that this experience of cosmic unity pre-existed their awareness of it. And this awareness makes stern, practical demands on their lives: their time in the desert will have been a preparation for the subversive activities of the Kingdom. Their own struggles in that dark time provide reserves of energy, and strength to resist the forces of evil, for they, too, like Jesus before them, know about the two Kingdoms – the Kingdom of Satan and the Kingdom of God.

The inward journey provides the resilience and strength

required for the work of the Kingdom of God; it is then possible to pray and do battle.

It might be asked why anyone should want to embark on such a journey with the possibility of such dubious rewards. The answer is that there is no real choice; for those who want to move from secondhand experience of religion to the reality, it is unavoidable. It is a journey usually undertaken more by women than by men; women, through their long history of suffering, in their waiting, vulnerability and tenacity, know more about this journey than men. Men have been expected to be the ones to organize, explain and get things done; there is little energy left for attention to the inner journey — so (with, of course, many exceptions), the religion of Protestantism has been just sensible and reasonable; it has mistrusted the areas of experience I have been hinting at. For them, talk of the inner journey is just pure regression; what they forget, of course, is that there is also a return journey.

Sometimes circumstances which formally have nothing to do with religion pitchfork a person into this journey. John was thirty-four, a computer technologist, married, with one child. One day he returned from work to find his Canadian-born wife had flown back to Ottawa: she felt that she just had to go home. Three days later he was made redundant. When I saw him, he was confused and angry with his wife, his former boss, himself and God. At the end of our talk he decided to go off and, as he said, "Sort himself out and get some counselling". Three months later he returned. His wife wanted a divorce; he had got a new job of sorts. He had been drinking, and he was on antidepressant pills.

Because he was talking to a priest, he wanted to discuss religious questions with me — "Where", he asked, "was God in all this?" I was surprised at the persistence of these questions, because he had never struck me as having more than a conventional interest in religion. So we agreed to meet regularly. He gave up the counselling. He threw away his pills. Very slowly he came to terms with his own weaknesses. John was an ambitious, aggressive and very confident person when I first met him. He was the sort of person to whom you couldn't tell anything. Now he discovered he could no longer order himself about. Together we began to explore the Christian mystics, and those who had chosen to live in the desert places. Slowly, he learnt to use the time of his solitude. (Very often when disturbances and upheavals occur, people find themselves alone, perhaps for the first time.) He began to study and practise techniques of breathing, meditation and contemplation. His collapse and disintegration – "I'm just going to pieces", he used to say – were followed by his desire to be made whole, and even to see a world which was also not fragmented or divided. He particularly liked many of the stories of the parties which Jesus both attended and sometimes talked about in his parables; for him they seemed a striking symbol of the restored "wholeness" of all creation. Eventually, he found he had forgiven himself and his wife, who had since remarried.

What was crucial for John was the awakening knowledge that he could trust himself in the dark times, that God was, as it were, beckoning him on through it all. He was able to digest and interpret his experience in that context of the incredibly rich, varied and generally unknown stories and teachings of the Christian monastic and mystical traditions. He sensed both the closeness and the nearness of God, and at the same time something of the unfathomable nature of God. John had, in fact, experienced the three classic phases of the mystical journey, first of purgation and purification, then of illumination through the darkness, and finally of transformation, where he discovered a freedom to become the sort of person he had it in him to be. He is now working with a development agency in Ethiopia.

I have written at length about John because the inner journey is not just for a few odd people. It can be for anyone whose life is suddenly disturbed and who wants to attend to that experience with all the seriousness that he can muster. The experience of hermits, monks and mystics paves the way and shines a light for the bewildered traveller.

There are, however, counterfeit forms of the inner journey which are dangerous and ultimately stand in opposition to the Kingdom of God. These are found in certain schools of meditation, some religious cults, some quasi-religious therapy groups based on the Human Potential movement, and some forms of transpersonal humanistic psychology. They promote a desire for an intense, spiritual experience which offers peace, harmony, bliss and ecstasy – invariably described as a transformation of consciousness. To know oneself is to know God, and vice versa. The stress is on the experience itself. It avoids abstract reasoning and analysis; it is about illumination, not action, about the experience of "the here and now", not about plotting the future. Moments of mystical unity are greatly treasured. Thus the physicist Fritjof Capra, sitting by the sea on a late summer afternoon, in watching the movement of the waves suddenly experiences the whole universe as a cosmic dance.

> I "saw" cascades of energy coming down from outer spaces
> in which particles were created and destroyed in rhythmic
> pulses. I "saw" the atoms of the elements and those of my
> body participating in this cosmic dance of energy: I felt its
> rhythms and I heard its sound, and at that moment I knew
> this was the Dance of Shiva.

The difficulty with this longing for spiritual experiences is that it frequently leads to a perception of the world as a prison from which the soul needs to escape and burst free – hence the interest in reincarnation and spiritualism, which are, incidentally, also frequently pervaded by narcissism. The teaching of self-discovery, self-healing, self-love and self-development are promulgated to secure inner tranquillity.

Narcissism breeds apathy and passivity which, should it and the pseudo-religious groups which feed on it begin to flourish, endangers the process of democracy and colludes with the fashionable view that our capacity for social and political change cannot be developed collectively.

This is not the inward journey of those who want to be part of the Kingdom of God. The process of transformation is not one which is just open to the self or God in the self, but to God in the world. The fact and presence of evil, the presence of suffering, the experience of lostness and nothingness cannot be bypassed. Rather, the inward journey enables those who make it to see with the eyes of God – both the anguish in the world, and whatever is found by way of beauty and grace. All forms of mysticism which do not lead to the doing of God's will "on earth as it is in heaven" are bogus.

Nevertheless, the Christian churches cannot ignore these movements; they are not a passing phenomenon. They have arisen because the churches seem to have denied the heart, the body and the spirit; Christianity seems to be worn out, existing on secondhand experiences and surviving on meaningless abstract dogmas.

The implications for a church which seriously encourages its members to take the inner journey are considerable.

The only way to approach those who have felt betrayed or cheated by Christianity is to express sorrow and penitence. It has been salutary over the years to listen to stories like this:

> Well, I was brought up in the Church of England, christened, and then confirmed when I was twelve. Went to several churches. The services were just boring. Nothing seemed to happen. We were always being asked to raise money and get more people to come. When I tried to ask the Vicar questions, he just looked nervous. There were so many words and complicated ideas to understand. I just wanted some experience of all these things we were hearing about. It was all a bit like school – so after a bit I left. No one seemed to mind.

For Western, British, English Christianity to attend to that critique means to acknowledge that "believing" is much more than an intellectual matter. It includes the exercise of the imagination and the body and the passions. It means, therefore, that doubt and uncertainty are an inevitable part of faith as I have tried to describe it in the account of my own journey. To deny this in the interest of some form of security or false certainty is to construct a religion which breeds intolerance, arrogance and cruelty, as all the forms of Fundamentalism – Muslim or Christian – illustrate.

What is therefore needed is to retrieve the experience of the monk and the mystic (and that of the prophet who is nourished by them) from the sidelines to the centre, so that those who are on the inner journey, or who might be prodded to start it, will be conscious of this rich soil on which we, mostly unawares, are standing. There is a need for people to emerge who can absorb this tradition, and interpret it.

But far more than that is required. Jung wrote, "Where are the great and wise men who do not merely talk about the meaning of life and the world, but really possess it?"

Generally not in the churches, is part of the answer to Jung's question. It is rare today to find such wisdom lived and distilled from hard experience of the desert places. It is natural to look towards the monastic orders for help, but many monks and nuns are themselves as confused as anyone else, as their orders experience decline in numbers and uncertainty as to new directions they should take. The clergy rarely show these qualities; we are a compulsive lot, trying to motivate people to come to church, raising money, keeping everybody happy. Like everybody else, we tend to seek our identity in being loved or admired or disliked; and because we never get enough admiration, we feel cheated, and frequently become angry and bitter. For anyone who undertakes the inner journey such compulsions disappear, for the identity of such a person is rooted in God, and in the light of the Kingdom.

It is probable that the wisdom I have spoken of will be found in new communities of the desert. In the West there are fewer and fewer wilderness areas, but these places are not the frontier posts of the Kingdom. It will be in the desert areas of our inner cities that such communities will be (and are being) born. Sharing the life of a neighbourhood, such a community may consist of as few as four or five people dedicated to the solitary life of silence and prayer, but in the context of a common life together, for however personal the journey is, there is no private way to God. Such people are an indispensable resource and guide for anyone dedicated to the Kingdom of God.

Perhaps these could be the sort of places today where wisdom will be found and, modest as they are, which could become laboratories of inspiration and hope for those for whom the service of the Kingdom of God matters above everything else.

4

Women and Men

There have always been women who have felt called to the priesthood, and clergy who have believed that women should be ordained but, because such belief was thought to be highly eccentric, their numbers were few and their voices muted. Increasingly, however, their numbers have grown and their voices cannot now be ignored.

Since 1986 the matter of women priests has been high on the agenda of Church Synods and Councils. In the Anglican Communion there are at least one thousand women priests from the Anglican Churches in Canada, Hong Kong, Kenya, New Zealand, the diocese of Polynesia in the South Pacific, and the U.S.A. All those who stand for election to the General Synod of the Church of England are expected to make their views known about women priests. Sooner or later a woman will be consecrated as a bishop, in the Anglican Communion.

Women have now organized themselves. In the last nine years in Britain, the Christian Women's Resource Group, the Christian Parity Group, Women in Theology, the Feminist Theology Group, and the Movement for the Ordination of Women, have been established. In 1984 a Roman Catholic Feminist Group was formed. Apart from the Movement for the Ordination of Women, which has a growing membership of over four thousand, these groups are small, consisting invariably of articulate, white, middle-class women; (beyond Britain there is a small, but significant, blooming of Christian Asian and African feminism).

Christian feminists are here to stay. All the traps and politicking of a conservative, patriarchal institution like the Roman Catholic Church or the Church of England will not deter them. There is something invincible about them. They have the clarity of those who have little or nothing to lose. Their alienation from the Church brings them both anguish and pain, as well as anger and indignation at their exclusion from it. Some of their liturgies speak of Exile. But anger and mourning are not all: their support and encouragement of each other, formed out of a longing and a determination for a regenerated and reformed Church where their insights and experience are treasured, gives Christian feminism a hope, an exuberance, a passion and a toughness which nothing can stop.

Traditionally, women are those who lay out the corpse for burial; they also help others to give birth, and it seems to me that Christian feminists are waiting at the door to help this process of death, burial and birth in our churches. It is a sad reflection that so many in the churches are unwilling to welcome this outpouring of female energy, and its prodigal imagination and intelligence, as women reconstitute themselves from their long history of exploitation.

What is remarkable is the speed with which Christian feminism has established itself, and the way in which its insights have invaded theological thinking, especially on the issue of the ordination of women. This is because the ground had been thoroughly prepared outside the churches in the feminist movement, first in America in the sixties, and later on in Britain.

Those who oppose the ordination of women justify their position by turning away from what is happening in society and back to history and tradition. They say that God chose to become a man, not a woman, and that men, not women, were chosen as apostles. They believe that when the Holy Communion is celebrated the priest stands in a special relationship to God: he is like a representative of Jesus, who at the Last Supper celebrated the first Holy Communion service. And since Jesus was a man, therefore the priest has to be a man. They argue that Jesus was precise about the instructions for this ceremony, that he chose bread and wine (not mutton and water – both were available at Passover time), that he chose himself to be the person who presided, and that his apostles were told to go on doing it in exactly the same way.

Thus for nearly two thousand years, this tradition has remained intact, and so, the argument goes, there is no reason to alter the situation now. Only a Council of all Christendom, the Orthodox Churches and the Roman Catholic Church, would have the authority to make such a drastic change, and for that there would have to be a clear, unambiguous consensus.

I see the matter differently on an altogether broader perspective. Men and women are fully and equally created in the image of God. They are not the same but they have equal potential to express themselves in that image and to be leaders in the Church. Jesus had many women friends and disciples. Women were the first to witness the Resurrection; they received the gifts of the Holy Spirit at Whitsun, and played a major part in establishing the first Christian churches.

A priest is not so much one who is set apart to be a replica of Jesus Christ – that should be true of all Christians – but as one who focuses and represents the Christian community. This consists of baptized women and men, and they form the Church – the body of Christ.

These are strictly theological arguments (there are others); and I need to stress straightaway that the case for the ordination of women does not depend on the secular grounds of sexual equality – an argument its opponents are very good at advocating – but on the infinitely deeper spiritual argument that the Church is deprived and unbalanced in its sacred ministry by the deliberate exclusion of women and the enormous contribution that they can bring in by their priesthood in so many areas of the ministry.

Even so, feminists are, of course, striving to obtain equal citizenship for women, in a world which for centuries has kept them in second place. No longer will they be defined and understood in relationship to men as subordinate and inferior to them. For some women, the spread of birth control has given them control of their bodies, as well as better education and opportunities for work. Women are a major untapped resource for a radical change in the direction of a participatory society where all are valued. In England 40 per cent of all wage and salary earners are women, and two out of five women wage earners have part-time jobs. These are usually the worst paid, with few fringe benefits or opportunities for promotion. And little is done for the million or so one-parent families, almost invariably headed by women, who have to be both mothers and wage earners. And not only in third world rural, agricultural economies do women have a crucial place, but also in our own industrial economy. Feminists rightly insist that more needs to be done to recognize these obvious but neglected facts.

Yet feminism is much more than about justice and equal opportunities. It presents a direct challenge to a world where for centuries men have ruled, and have said what women should and could do and be. Within feminism there are many divisions and conflicts, but the fundamental impulse behind it is a new, urgent, moral awareness of what it does mean and could mean to be a woman in a community of women and men in equal partnership. It is a new movement of the human spirit, transcending national, racial and religious boundaries; it is a sign of the presence of the Kingdom of God – a sign of hope for the transformation of society.

Christian feminists grounded in the secular feminist movement also look to their own experience as Christians. They are alienated by a God who, in the Bible, in the teachings of the Church and in its worship, is described almost exclusively as Father, Lord, Judge, King – one who is arbitrary, supreme, requiring obedience and submission to the male hierarchy.

Even if it is said that such crude, anthropomorphic ways of envisaging God are in reality only pointers to God, and fatherhood is not to be taken literally, still the masculine image of God is so deeply embedded in Christian culture that such explanations are merely the sophisticated claims of men who want to keep the situation exactly as it is.

Christianity is an historical religion. It did not come into being through our own reasoning or some arcane spiritual experience but as a piece of history, limited and partial; then God was understood predominantly in male imagery, male symbolism, male language, and, because the Incarnation of Jesus Christ is fundamental and for Christians for all time, it is difficult for some women to feel at home in this setting. So it is possible to think of a black Christ on the Cross, indeed any male figure, but it is more difficult to place a woman on the Cross, and say that was Jesus.

Yet to focus and restrict the meaning of the mission of Jesus in terms of his maleness leads to the logical conclusion that the salvation he offered was just for Jewish males. When the early Church debated the meaning of the life and death and resurrection of Jesus (though debate is too mild a description; there was much ferocious quarrelling), it agreed ultimately that the focus of the Incarnation was not maleness, but humanity itself – that was the essence or the heart of the historical event of Jesus of Nazareth. If this is so, then it is possible and legitimate to consider a woman being portrayed on the Cross, as happened in the Cathedral of St John the Divine, New York, when Edwina Sandys' sculpture, "Christa", was placed in the cathedral during Holy Week of 1985.

Meanwhile, Christian feminists are alienated from the history of Christianity – from the patriarchs, judges, kings and prophets in the Old Testament, to Jesus, Peter and Paul, and then to the Popes, Cardinals, Archbishops, Bishops, Priests and Ministers they see the history of the Church as being made by men. Women have been the invisible presence, listening, acquiescing, collaborating with men, but almost always in a largely subservient role.

Therefore Christian feminists are alienated from the Church's doctrines. Early Christian and mediaeval teaching on the nature of men and women certainly reinforced their subordinate position. Aristotle's philosophy underlies the thinking on Women of St Augustine and Thomas Aquinas: women were regarded as deficient, emotionally, psychologically and spiritually.

St Augustine wrote:

The woman together with her own husband is the image of God, so that the substance may be one image, but when she is referred to separately in her capacity of help-mate, which regards the woman herself alone, then she is not the image of God; but as regards the man alone, he is the image of God as fully and completely as when the woman too is joined with him.

Such sentiments, however eminent the author of them, can only be regarded as repugnant and ridiculous today.

*

So it was believed that women were merely the containers in which the baby grew, and that this new human being's life was due entirely to the male. It was hoped that the male would reproduce himself, and that when something went wrong (perhaps due to a breeze, according to Thomas Aquinas) a female child would be born. These views show how the female is understood to be included in the male, who alone exemplifies what it is to be human. As biology this is of course nonsense, but the subordination of women is still very much in evidence. The Bishop of London, for example, is not alone in believing that women can never be priests because the initiative in creation comes from God, and is revealed in God's Son Jesus Christ and shared with men; women, so this argument goes, are invited to respond in obedience and so complement God's and man's initiative.

But this is not all. If at this somewhat abstract level women are defined in the light of who men are, the definition is compounded by men's attitude to women. There is a long Christian tradition which says that women, through Eve, are the source of wickedness in the world. They are the supreme seducers and tempters. Men's fear of the sexual power of women luring them away from virtue is a stock theme of early Christian and mediaeval teaching. So Abbot Odo of Cluny, encouraging celibate clergy to be resolute when faced by the seductive charms of women, writes:

> The beauty of a woman is only skin deep. If men could only see what is beneath the flesh and penetrate below the surface with eyes like a Brestian lynx, they would be nauseated just to look at women, for all this feminine charm is nothing but phlegm, blood, humus, gall. Just imagine all that is hidden in nostrils, throat and stomach ... We are all repelled to touch vomit and ordure even with our fingertips. How then can we ever want to embrace what is merely a sack of rottenness?

It seems incredible to us today that devout and holy men could be guilty of such terrible prejudice, but these opinions were indeed all too common, and although such language could never be used now, the residual effect of these attitudes is still prevalent in the minds of many clergy opposed to the ordination of women.

Elsewhere, St Jerome says woman is the door of the devil and the way of iniquity. St Maximus calls the woman the shipwreck of man. St Athanasius the Sinaite calls her the clothed serpent, the spear in the heart. St Bonaventure says that the woman clothed in her finery is a well sharpened word of the devil.

These views seem absurd and extreme, but I easily recognize what they are about: they are a clear case of projection by men. Because of the depth, strength and confusion of sexual feelings, and the difficulty of bringing together the spiritual and the erotic (religion and sex), an easy way out for us is simply to deny this confusion and put all the blame on women. Such hostility and misogyny is hardly concealed. Another way to avoid these difficulties is to place women on pedestals. Thus men idealize women. Virginity and motherhood are exalted. Purity is all. Either way, so women tell me, they lose: they are either treated as sexual objects or their sexuality is denied. Eve, Mary – the Pure Virgin and Mother – and the Witch, the one who exercises mysterious power over men and creation, all find their place in the Christian tradition. Many Christian feminists have told me how much they resent the way in which they are continually and consistently understood and described in the shadow of the male – for if one thing is certain they are finding their identity, their strength, their centre beyond this shadow.

But what shall a woman do as she leaves this shadow and stands in another light? Some voices in the Church will say that she is mistaken – Christian feminism, so the argument goes, is yet another example of the Church's selling out to contemporary liberal fads. A woman's job is to respect the Church's teaching and tradition; if she starts to tamper with either, then whether she knows it or not, indeed wants to or not, this signals the end of the Christian religion. Feminism will be the undoing of the Church. A woman's place is in the home; the fulfilment of her true nature is to create a peaceful, happy home in the midst of a threatening society – a place to which the man can retreat and recover. Just as Mary is portrayed, in "Once in Royal David's

City", as mild, and lowly and gentle, so Christian women have enough to do being dutiful, self-effacing, self-sacrificing, hard working and obedient to their husbands. Women themselves are the first to feel threatened by the voices of Christian feminists, since not only have they happily all these years arranged the flowers, made the coffee and run Sunday Schools (what other option was open to them?), but now their understanding of their role is being undermined by those whom they regard as fanatical extremists.

But it is difficult to see how Christian feminists will knuckle down and become good little girls or sweet old ladies. Some will abandon Christianity; others already have. If, as Mary Daly said, where God is male then male is God, then Christianity is alien to them. They move beyond the Christian religion seeking a new (or very ancient) Mother Goddess, but this gender reversal only establishes a new dualism where men are put in the secondary role once occupied by women. Those women who have abandoned the Church, often with much anger and bitterness, are those whom feminist detractors regard as typical. Such women see Christianity as a worn-out religion whose adherents worship a God who is at best superfluous, and at worst destructive. In fact, they are few in number, although they possibly represent many more women who will not and cannot have anything to do with patriarchal religion.

If this is the case, and if those who have abandoned Christianity are persuasive enough, then that does spell the beginning of the end, because sooner or later women will get to hear of it and believe it. Some will quite angrily, some in sorrow, and others will quietly, close the church door behind them. Well, they say, that was Christianity. And all that will be left will be tiny, like-minded clubs which meet to preserve old rituals and old buildings.

But there are many women who continue with much patience to belong to Christian communities. Suffocated by the way male leadership is exercised and decisions are made; frustrated by the encompassing male shadow which casts such gloom around their growing central awareness of themselves as persons and as women, they struggle to relate their consciousness and experience as women to the consciousness of their Christian faith and experience of the Church. Such weaving of connections (where they exist) has forced open the bastion of theology – for centuries a pastime of white, academic, Western, educated and privileged men; up till now it is they and they alone who interpreted, explained and taught the Christian faith. This activity, this movement of the heart as well as the head, focuses the challenge of Christian feminism to the churches – about belief in God, about Jesus Christ, about attitudes, about the nature of men and women and about the life, organization and structures of the Church. The novelist, Monica Furlong, describes this movement "as fundamental as the discovery of the early Church that the truth of Christ was meant for Gentiles as well as Jews ... It is as if a new source of energy had suddenly discovered itself in the Church, like a spring of water ... bubbling up, turning into a large pool and gradually into a river irrigating a dry countryside."

Perhaps a more pedestrian image conveys more accurately some of the work that Christian feminists are doing; it is that of dismantling, and exploration – discarding the patriarchal masculine images and symbols and then digging up long forgotten ways, and possibly discovering new ways of speaking of God. Christian history is also being ransacked to see if there are any treasures which women can discover; but such dismantling is in its early stages.

Some women feel that the tradition of, say, speaking about God as Mother is so fitful, so thin, that in their exploration they have to try to stand over against Christianity, and yet still find a way to remain within it.

Others begin to want to discard altogether what they see as the crude, anthropomorphic way of talking about God as Father or Mother. Parental images for some feminists speak of domination, whereas they seek for ways of speaking, thinking and of experiencing God which empower one another. Some speak of God as coming into being among them, yet also over against them as one who in their prayers they address as "Thou". Margaret Bearlin, writing on Theological Imperatives for Christian Involvement in peace and disarmament, puts it like this:

If our concern is with the love of a creating, sustaining, sanctifying, indwelling spirit for the life and wholeness of the world, we will be caught up and enlivened by the images of the Spirit, desiring to break through in reconciling, whole-making love between all people, all beings and all things in the universe. This God (if we can so name) is inside, within us, even under us, in the depths of our being, empowering us, flowering out from, between us and all things both immanent and transcendent.

What is happening here and elsewhere in the thinking and corporate reflection of Christian feminism is a recasting, and a transformation of the Christian tradition.

Others believe that it is necessary to stay closer to the tradition and keep the understanding of the Fatherhood of God, but seek to understand it in another way. This is the Fatherhood of God directly related to the Cross. Thus if God is remote, unfeeling, judging his disobedient people, then that is not a true pattern of fatherhood. For the Cross shows God the Creator becoming helpless and powerless amongst the wickedness and evil of men and women; God is the one who suffers with all in God's Creation. And this God is disclosed in the man Jesus, in the mysterious events of the Passion and Crucifixion and Resurrection – but also, as we have seen, in his preaching and living out the good news about the Kingdom of God. Here the model of male power and male patriarchy disintegrates. A new image of Fatherhood is waiting to come to birth which questions our own assumptions about Fatherhood and Motherhood. Perhaps it will be possible to say, with Dame Julian of Norwich, the thirteenth-century English mystic, that "as truly God is our Father, so just as truly is he our Mother".

Alongside these explorations women are returning to the Bible. Even if the biblical record assumes patriarchy as the norm, and the history of women has been either suppressed, forgotten or ignored, there is enough in the biblical story for women to reclaim – not only as significant followers of Jesus, but also as leaders in the first Christian communities. These discoveries are invigorating; they add a rich dimension to the collective memories of the Church, and enliven our historical imagination. These memories are both dangerous and hopeful – dangerous because they are reminders of the consistent oppression of women, and hopeful because they remind women (and men) of other possibilities. Here are two examples, neither of them well known: the first is from the Old Testament, from the beginning of the Book of Exodus, and the birth of Moses. The midwives were ordered by Pharaoh to murder all the baby boys; they refused to do so because they "feared God". Later the baby Moses was placed in a box by the river. His mother, sister, and Pharaoh's daughter saved Moses – both the midwives and the women (from different races) being "disobedient" to Pharaoh. If later God was acting through Moses to deliver his people, so women at the start of the story of the Exodus were the first independent agents of God.

The second example is from the New Testament – from Luke 11:27–28:

> While he was speaking thus, a woman in the crowd called out, "Happy the womb that carried you and the breasts that suckled you!" he rejoined, "No, happy are those who hear the word of God and keep it." (N.E.B.)

Most of the commentaries I have read (written by men) stress that Jesus just corrected the woman. Others use the text to correct excessive veneration of Mary. But what in fact is happening is that Jesus is rejecting the stereotype of woman as primarily a reproductive being. At that time women were honoured if they had children, and preferably boys. If they were barren, they were pitied. Their position in society was defined by their ability to procreate. But Jesus rejects this understanding – to him, a woman was one who "hears the Word of God and does it".

Such interpretations are not special pleading. They are there in the texts. And they have been made (and could only have been made) by women. Thus on the fringes of the Church, in small groups and modest meetings, this thinking out, reflecting, modifying and searching is going on. Women share their common experience and begin to see how a fresh understanding of the nature of God can be a new source of hope and healing, how the partial, distorted and limited picture of God can be replaced by one including a vision of the masculine and feminine within women and men, and within God.

That is enough theology. Leaving aside the critical questions of doctrine and believing, how is Christian feminism being received, and what do Christian communities begin to look like where feminists begin to feel at home?

Janet Morley, in her contribution "The Faltering Words of Men – Exclusive Language in the Liturgy" (published in the collection of Essays – *Feminine in the Church*, edited by Monica Furlong)[1], tells of the reaction of *Times* readers to the United Church of Canada's document "Guidelines for Inclusive Language", which received a lot of press coverage and a *Times* leader. The issues raised by the document deal with the language of the liturgy, particularly, for example, when, through the gratuitous use of "men", women feel excluded. Janet Morley was intrigued by the depth of feeling this matter aroused. Some saw such tinkering with the language as trivial and pedantic; others objected on aesthetic grounds (try putting "person" wherever "man" is mentioned in the Alternative Service Book). Others spoke of emasculating, impoverishing and murdering the language (strong words themselves). Others described the inclusion of "Mother" and "Father" to address God as positively Satanic, since it was tampering with their fundamentals of Christianity. The ferocity of these reactions suggests that those who wished to hold on to the sexist, exclusive language of ancient and contemporary services are frightened – so frightened that no changes could be even considered by them, quite regardless of the suffering and pain which it brought to their sisters in the faith.

The language of the liturgy is, of course, a crucial element in this debate. Worship, whether we like it or not, shapes the consciousness of worshippers; it recalls our common heritage, reinforces the identity of Christian communities, legitimates attitudes and so prescribes behaviour. Women experience such worship as yet another way which intensifies their alienation from religion, and to them it is invariably another act of domination. The fears that inclusive language creates arise from the projections men have made of their attitudes to women. In other words, those parts of men's experience which men find difficult to handle with respect to their religious beliefs and aspirations – their sexuality, the sense of their bodies, and their weakness and vulnerability – are split off and projected on to women, whom men then punish, both for showing those qualities they resist in themselves and also for their denial and splitting of these qualities.

Women become scapegoats. They bear, as they have always done, the fears and anxieties of men. If worship is to speak to God in God's holiness and wholeness, then these splits have to be faced and have to be healed. Until exclusive language is banned women will never be at home in the Church, and men burdened with the sense of exemplifying true humanity will neither discover their own beauty or true masculinity; above all, they will lack the quality found supremely in God and in women – compassion; they will not know how "to suffer with".[2]

Christian feminism generates strong feelings, and strong fears. However sympathetic men may be to this phenomenon it is still disturbing (and very difficult to write about). Most of us will have to embark on a journey of undoing and unlearning, particularly those who hold power in Church – bishops and clergy. Old habits die hard. Some of these are being slaves to thinking processes, and ignoring emotions and feelings. Our fear of our sexuality and our need to control every situation has to be addressed. We have to come to terms with our bodily nature and our capacity for tenderness and vulnerability. We have to understand that our bodies are not just things to be ordered about, or ignored, but are an integral and obvious part of our "presence". It is the disembodiment of men (particularly of some clergy) which so often prevents them from being fully present in situations where the human response, the sense of another's presence, is required – more than any time, words or prayers.

Men's response to Christian feminism ought to be one of penitence and shame that they have imposed upon the world such a partial, distorted view of God. There are plenty of opportunities for penitence. It is strange when in public discussions about the case for or against the ordination of women, for example, women soon disappear from the debate. Institutional questions take over at once, particularly among those who oppose the ordination of women; anxieties are expressed about the unity of the Church, and relationships with the Roman Catholic or Orthodox Churches. The debate shifts at once to the abstract level. But that is just the point at which men should remind the Church of the shameful history of the way it has treated women, and often still continues to treat them today.

Earlier I spoke of women who felt suffocated by the way churches made decisions. Christian communities which pay proper attention to this frustration will examine carefully the way power is exercised. Women see male power as consciously or unconsciously based on a superior sense that men have over women; it is a symptom of the way that men have provided the norm for what is right. Male power operates from a hierarchical base. Bishops wear "crowns" (mitres); sit on episcopal thrones; are addressed as "My Lord"; some speak of ruling their diocese. Women (and some men!) perceive such a way of exercising power as uncaring and aggressive.

But where Christian feminism begins to be experienced, another power is discerned. It is anti-hierarchical. It is communal – even, to some men's eyes, anarchic; its purpose is to nurture and sustain a community in which each one has the greatest opportunity for self realization within the context of the whole. It seeks, therefore, to be a power which encourages and empowers each person. It is reflective. The power of the question is valued. The power of Christian feminists as it begins to work in churches promotes forms of leadership whereby the process, the way things are done, is as important as the outcome. They seek not to dominate or control, but to develop collaborative ways of working; they may, if they are in an official leadership role, point out the result of a decision were it to be taken, but they would not enforce such a decision on others. In this ministry, or service to the Christian community, ancient meanings are recovered; for example, it is far closer to the understanding and practice of Jesus's leadership, where the first will be last and the last first.[3]

No one should underestimate the difficulties involved in

exercising this sort of power; it has eluded institutional Christianity ever since the beginning of the Church. Moreoever, the vested interest of men to hold on to their own power means that there is a long struggle ahead. Because the "old" power is so strong, the danger remains that women would be and are being assimilated into the patriarchal structure, leaving them unaltered.

Therefore in both America and in Britain, there are women who gather together to become an "alternative church". Those who join such communities discover solidarity, compassion, affirmation and celebration, which is missing in even the most generous of male-dominated churches. Such communities are criticized for lacking the "fullness of the Church"; yet women say that the hierarchical male Church also lacks fullness. Others say this is colonialism in reverse. But no one criticizes, say, the people of Africa coming together as "colonialism in reverse". All that is happening, and will need to happen, is that women are getting together on their own for their own spiritual survival, both as women and as Christian persons.

The more I have listened to women, and learnt from them, the more I have come to see that we – the men – are the problem. We find it difficult to let women find their own identity; we often express irritation and anger at "strident and hysterical" women – barely concealing our confusion and anxiety.

What is it then that men can do – apart from developing a fine conscience about their own attitudes and actions – both personally and publicly? We can do much to attack pornography and prostitution. Women's bodies have been battered, raped, sterilized, mutilated – for male purposes and male ends. Therefore, men have to take on other men – not to defend women, but to get other men to see how much they brutalize women. It is a difficult task, and it has hardly begun.

Eventually, it must be possible to find a new form of partnership between women and men, when both will empower one another in the service of the Kingdom. But it is work for many generations.

5

Jesus, Muhammad, Buddha and the Kingdom – Something New for the Human Spirit[1]

The religion in which a person believes, and to which he adheres, usually depends upon where he was born. Born of Muslim parents in Egypt, you would be a Muslim. In Burma you would be a Buddhist; in India, born of Hindu parents you would be a Hindu. Born of Christian parents in Europe, North America or Australasia you would be a Christian. If in Britain you have a "conversion" experience, it is more likely to be to Christianity rather than to another religion.

These obvious statements raise a barrage of disturbing and difficult questions: how can one account for the diversity of religions? How can God be one yet worshipped in so many different ways? Do religions have anything in common, and if so, can anything be learnt from them? Are they all equally true or false? What place do they have in the Kingdom of God? These questions are disturbing, not least because until comparatively recently the major world religions lived in total geographical isolation from one another.

This is no longer so. In Britain, for example, there are one and a half million Muslims, more than the combined membership of the Baptist and Methodist churches. The Muslim community, and the Hindu and Jewish communities, do everything to ensure that their distinct identities are preserved by the observance of their religions. Thus, the United Kingdom Islamic Mission arranges a programme of supplementary education. Four thousand Muslim children receive supplementary education in three hundred schools and centres. Here Arabic is taught, so the children can read the Koran and learn about their parents' culture.

Leaders of the major religions want regular access to radio and television, particularly at their festival times; they resent the Christian monopoly of religious broadcasting. The United Kingdom Christian Handbook shows a steady decline in numbers among the main Christian denominations (except for the Baptists, which hold their own), but Buddhists, Hindus, Krishna followers and Sikhs are increasing.

Britain is therefore a multi-faith society, and that is what makes attention to those questions so pressing, and so difficult; for until recently interest in other religions was considered a mildly eccentric pastime. But now the shelves of any reputable bookshop display translations of the Koran, the Bhagavad Gita, the Tao-Te Ching, the Dhammapada – as well as the Bible. Commentaries, explanations and introductions to the Eastern religions are as popular as books by Christian theologians. The 1960s rush of interest in the Eastern religions has evolved into a steadier and more critical interest in world religions. It has become difficult to raise religious questions in schools and colleges solely in a Christian context.

In spite of strenuous and sustained efforts, with the presence of Christianity in every continent and almost every nation, Christians still only number about 30 per cent of the world's population, and, if the present population explosion continues in non-Western, non-Christian nations, by the year 2000 Christians will number about 16 per cent of the world population. Christian converts have usually come from cultures where the hold of religion has almost disappeared, or from polytheistic or animistic religions. Christianity has made little headway with living religions such as Islam, Hinduism, or Buddhism.

How should the churches respond to the presence of these world religions? There are some who are fearful that Britain will lose its Christian identity. They want the Church, and particularly the established Church of England (together with the monarchy), to provide both an identity and a common store of values, which would allow our pluralist society to flourish.

Without this, so the argument goes, there is little to hold the hotch potch of groups and conflicting interests together, and the way is open to instability and disintegration. They see themselves as "hosts" to immigrant communities; they welcome them, but want to keep separate from them.

Then there are those who see the presence of so many religions as an opportunity for evangelism. This has been the traditional attitude of mainline Protestantism and, until recently, Roman Catholicism. The Protestant believes there is no salvation outside Jesus Christ, and that Jesus, the Son of God, the second person of the Trinity, is the unique and exclusive revelation of God. For centuries, the Roman Catholic Church had proclaimed "outside the Church, no Salvation". If there is to be any meeting with other faiths, it is only to understand them, so that they can be more swiftly brought to repentance, and accept Jesus Christ as their saviour.

There is a third and more constructive response, and that is to welcome the truth – that Britain today is multi-racial and multi-faith. The opportunity therefore presents itself to discover how different groups with different religions can live together and learn from one another.

It depends on how we view the stranger. Our natural inclination is to keep the stranger at a distance, so that a relationship of superiority and inferiority is maintained. I once heard a well educated Indian woman speaking to a local Mothers' Union. She was speaking of her country, of its colossal problems of poverty and over-population, and of the valiant attempts to do something about them. When it was time for questions, a white middle-aged Englishwoman asked, "Do you think there will ever come a time when they will be civilized like us?" The woman coming from the country of Buddha and Gandhi paused for a moment, and then said, "Yes, and I dread it". (She could have added that when the British were savages, there was already a tradition of philosophy, religion and learning in India.)

But to recognize the other as a stranger, someone you do not know, and cannot understand, could also be the chance to recognize that you do not know or understand yourself. It is as if to say that as well as being an individual, a member of a family, a community, a nation and a race, "I" as an individual will never fully understand myself as long as there are strangers in the world. This recognition that we do not know or understand ourselves is threatening and alarming. Nevertheless, once the step is taken to welcome the strangers then it is possible to begin a search for common values which we can share together.

The welcoming of the stranger is also not just an individual matter, but the recognition of our interdependence and need for collaboration and co-operation on a global scale – economically, ecologically, politically, so that a new world order can somehow come about. The urgency and difficulty of such a task is obvious in the light of the precarious nature of "peace" in the world today.

A children's story, "Dinosaurs and all that rubbish", expresses such a vision of universality. A man devastates the earth so that he can build a rocket and travel to another planet. After he leaves, some dinosaurs, who had been asleep under the ground for years, emerge, and rebuild the earth into a planet of abundance and life. The man discovers that all the planets are barren. Then one day he discovers a planet green and lush, cared for by dinosaurs. He recognizes that it is the earth. He asks, begs, for just a small plot for himself. "No", says a dinosaur.

> Not a part of it
> But all of it,
> It is all yours
> But it is also mine.
> Remember that.
> This time the earth belongs to everyone.
> Not part of it to certain people
> But all of it to everyone
> To be enjoyed and cared for.

Such a vision will only begin to be realized if it is sustained, enriched and shaped by religious symbols which cherish the value of the individual, the primacy of justice and love, and the sustaining presence of God in creation.

All religions, in principle, value love for the neighbour. All contain symbols of the unity of all humankind and creation. It is true, of course, that the religions have contributed, and still contribute, to ugly conflicts and divisions in the world, but, if they could begin to respect each other, learn from one another, and create among themselves some sense of a world fellowship, they might help in the search for a more stable and united world.

These reflections on the personal and planetary, global implications of welcoming the stranger show that the multi-faith, multi-racial society is not just something to be endured, but an essential ingredient for the development and future of the planet. They provide the background for any positive understanding of the diversity of religions.

This view was given encouragement in 1961, when the great Roman Catholic theologian, Karl Rahner, published his study on Christianity and world religions. It was a watershed for the Roman Catholic Church. Here was a new recognition of the presence and grace of God in all the major religious traditions. More than that, Karl Rahner said that there was Salvation in other religions; that in a hidden, indirect and implicit way, it was the work of Christ. Thus a deeply religious Buddhist who may know little or nothing about Christianity or the Gospel would, on this argument, have accepted Christianity had he encountered it. He is therefore what Rahner calls an "anonymous Christian". This approach advocates that God is saving people within other religions because they are potentially Christian at heart.

The concept of the "anonymous Christian" was a huge step in the recognition of the riches of other religions, and the acknowledgement that all religions produce prophets, saints, teachers and devout women and men who reflect the one God. In honouring them, the Roman Catholic Church also managed to hold on to the traditional teaching that salvation came through Jesus Christ and him alone.

And this is the issue which confronts anyone who bothers about developing some understanding between Christianity and other religions. For if Jesus Christ is the unique, absolute, exclusive, definitive revelation of God, then the superiority of

Christianity is assured (at least in the eyes of Christians), and all other religions must be defective.

There is, therefore, an urgent task for the Church to continue the work of Karl Rahner, and to seek to understand Christianity in the light of the presence and witness of the historic, ancient religions. It is not easy; time and again the New Testament affirms that Jesus is "the only begotten Son of God" (John 14:6), or that there is "no other name" by which we can be saved (Acts 4:12).

These and many other texts are quite clear, and the writers and the Christian communities for whom they wrote meant what they said. Yet the language of "one and only" is not – in the Bible – the language of metaphysics, theology and Christian doctrine; that only emerged later.

The "exclusive" language used about Jesus Christ is much more a reminder of the messy, violent and exhilarating way in which the Christian Church grew, adapting to the world of the Roman Empire, gradually coming to terms with the fact that the end of the world was not going to happen (as the earlier Christians expected). The human, historical perspective is, at least, a start in coming to terms with the "one and only" language.

It is, first of all, the language of survival; the earliest Christian communities were tiny, quarrelsome, invariably poor groups (usually extended households) in large cities. They were in danger of either being wiped out by the Roman Empire or of being absorbed into the pagan religions round about them. Inevitably, they had to arm themselves with a crystal clear identity; in this way the language of "one and only" says much more about the life of the earliest churches than about the person and nature of Jesus.

The language is also that of witness, testimony or confession; it is the language of lovers. When someone says of his or her lover, "You are the only person for me", that speaks of commitment; it is not a dogmatic, metaphysical statement, but the expression of an immediate and strong emotion. The earliest Christian communities – living out of a mysterious "big bang" religious experience of the Risen Christ present among them through the power of the Spirit – interpreted Jesus Christ in astonishingly different ways – as the prophet who came to announce the Kingdom and warn of the impending judgement, as the bearer of God's Wisdom, as the wonder miracle worker, as the promised Messiah, to name just four. These various impressionistic pictures were not authoritative; no one response claimed pride of place. There were probably others of which we do not know.

Much of the intellectual, theological work on these matters has now been done. But it is not accessible. No theologian, historian, film-maker or television producer has yet made this period of history available, in all its untidiness, mystery and energy. But when this human dimension is glimpsed, it is possible to catch something of what the exclusive language is about. And ultimately, Christian commitment is the same today as then. Anyone whose heart has been empowered or whose mind has been lit by responding to the call to serve God's Kingdom which Jesus sounds, will also feel the urge to speak in such terms.

No one should underestimate the difficulties in the perplexing and daunting task of what is called "inter-faith dialogue" – which means sharing beliefs and experiences in order that each may learn and grow from one another. It is an activity which demands staying power and, above all, imagination.

Imagination is the key. It involves a "mental" and "spiritual" approach of "passing over" and then "returning". It is as if I left England and lived for many years in a remote village in the Andes. During that time, I retained my Englishness, but I also became part of the village community, first observing and then participating in its customs and traditions. On my return to London, I noticed things I had not noticed before – how noisy the traffic was, how people did not greet each other. Furthermore, my time in the Andes had illuminated and changed me.

To "pass over" into the experience of another religion is to allow the stories, symbols and images of that religion to "work" on me. In the course of that "journey" I will have assimilated those stories which moved my heart; I will have discovered whether the religion makes sense, and is satisfying intellectually.

I will soon know whether it is a religion which liberates or enslaves its followers. The "return" journey will have inevitably enriched my perceptions and attitudes to my own religion. The process I have described is not just for experts, for anyone who is rooted in a religious tradition can experience it. It is the characteristic of attentive listening which is required above all.

Canon Max Warren, a former General Secretary of the Church Missionary Society, in an address in 1958 put this in words which have since become famous:

> Our first task in approaching another people, another culture, another religion is to take off our shoes, for the place we are approaching is holy. Else we may find ourselves treading on men's dreams. More serious still, we may forget that God was here before our arrival.

The process of sharing and mutual education can only take place if there is an agreement that no one person has the right to claim that all the truth is only on his or her side. Beliefs may have to be abandoned. Conversion to new beliefs may emerge.

But the most effective way for different religious traditions to enrich each other's religion is to work together for the values of the Kingdom of God – the end of oppression, the removal of injustice and the promotion of a just and peaceful society. If the world religions in Britain can begin to work together, locally and nationally, there is the tiny beginning of a new common identity for the whole nation which celebrates a multi-racial, multi-faith community.

It is far too early to say where such a process of listening, reflecting, sharing and working together will lead. It is not a priority of the British churches. Few theologians know anything about other religions. Interfaith studies are not taught at theological colleges. Interfaith matters rarely surface in the Church's councils and synods, still remaining a concern for enthusiasts and specialists. And Christianity is very impoverished by it. For there is just enough experience to see something new for the human spirit which is slowly, tentatively, beginning to emerge.

Those who have worked and lived for the mutual sharing and learning from different traditions point to a new understanding of truth. Truth needs other truths. Each religion has something unique and distinctive about it. Each truth is complemented by another. Each truth is paradoxical. Those who speak of God in personal terms yet move beyond to silence. Those who speak of the presence of the Kingdom of God, yet recognize that it is also near at hand. The different strands of tradition are mutually enriching. Those who are drawn to the mystical traditions need the prophets; the prophets need the mystics, otherwise their prophetic words will become harsh and unlovely. More formally, the doctrine of the Trinity needs the Islamic insistence on the oneness of God; the impersonal emptiness of Buddhism needs the Jewish/Christian experience of the God who calls. We can hardly grasp the implications of the complementary insights of different religions. Does it point to the eventual emergence of one world religion? I doubt it. Cultural, economic and political interests alone would prevent this; and anyhow, it is the riches, and the character, of each tradition which separately enhance the whole.

But if there are some adventurous spirits, and some adventurous churches who, as they engage in experiencing other religions, reassess their own perceptions and experience, then as the assimilation of insights, experience and practice happens, so Christianity will grow, evolve and shine with a steadier, brighter light.

This deep assimilation has always been a feature of Christian history. Christianity has been changing and evolving since its inception. There is no unchanging Gospel encased in a capsule, untouched by human minds. Thus when Christianity moved away from Jewish soil to the furthest points of the Roman Empire, it was transformed. When St Thomas Aquinas constructed his vast theological edifice on the basis of the "pagan" philosophy of Aristotle, Christianity was again transformed. And today, Christianity is trying to come to terms with the legacy of the Enlightenment.

Now Christianity could be on the verge of yet another transformation. Its centre has already shifted from Europe and North America to the culture and religions of the Third World. Here there is the chance of a renewed faith (though still recognizable as Christian, yet genuinely new) as it interacts with Islam, Hinduism, Buddhism. How much of these ancient religions will be absorbed into the thinking and practice of Christianity, only time will tell, but if it fails to seize this opportunity, Christianity will die.

Western, European, British, English Christianity sometimes seems so played out and exhausted. This is because it feeds on itself. Nothing illustrates this better than the Christian ecumunical movement. In spite of all the reports and studies and discussions, and the prodigious energy of many theologians and church leaders, ecumenism has run out of steam and has achieved very little. Yet the opportunities for evolution, growth and transformation are present in Britain, provided the churches seriously and deliberately – locally, nationally and internationally – engage in the process of listening and sharing and working closely with those of other faiths who are our partners and our friends.

6

Reforming Worship

Churches are voluntary organizations; they have to concern themselves with funding and membership drives. They have their fair share of squabbles and internal politicking. But when Christians gather together to share bread and wine, to pray, to sing hymns, to listen to sermons and the reading of the Bible, they are engaged in activities which are distinctive; they say to one another, as it were, "This is who we are, and whose we are, where we have come from and where our future lies". The character and identity of that group, that congregation, is defined and declared and affirmed. Further, the activity of worship shapes the understandings, perceptions and values of its members. Worship is therefore an activity of great significance.

It is strange then that words like "going to church" or "church services" or "worship" evoke not expectation or anticipation, but boredom. For that is what many say: church services are boring, creepy, deadly.

As listeners to the radio and viewers of television, our critical faculties are highly developed. Today's audience has high expectations of communication, which clergy usually fail to meet – churches are often cold, uncomfortable, invasive of privacy, musically and visually unsophisticated. We remember being forced to endure going to church as children. It speaks of a world we are glad to be able to leave behind.

There have, of course, been changes in our patterns of worship designed to meet these criticisms. In 1980 the Church of England published the Alternative Service Book, which is the official alternative to the Book of Common Prayer, and is authorized for use until 1990. (All the main-line denominations have now revised their service books.) The new prayer book was not imposed on the church. Discontent with the narrowness of the

73

Book of Common Prayer had been expressed for over a hundred years. Committees, lengthy debates and many discussions ensured wide consultation, eventually leading to an agreement about the text which the extremes of the Church of England (the Anglo-Catholics and the conservative Evangelicals) could use with good conscience (which is certainly not so with the Prayer Book).

The Alternative Service Book has had a mixed reception. Many clergy were relieved to have a book which was flexible and would meet the needs of their congregations. But there was also fierce opposition from conservative Anglicans who felt that the roots of their faith had been severed. There was a dotty debate in the House of Lords, revealing some anti-clericalism targeted at trendy vicars. There were petitions signed by eminent persons, and letters to *The Times*. But the speed with which the Alternative Service Book has been accepted and used throughout thousands of parishes showed something of the discontent and dissatisfaction with the 1662 Book of Common Prayer.

However, the Alternative Service Book is itself most unsatisfactory. In spite of all the energy so many put into its preparation for so many years, the end result is a huge missed opportunity. The book will become increasingly a liability for congregations, who will either slowly abandon it in favour of some "do it yourself" worship or even return to using the Prayer Book (which itself is unusable on a regular basis; it belongs very much to a time which is not ours).

There are two major criticisms of the Alternative Service Book. The first is that the book encourages a sense that our churches are exclusive clubs. Thus the practice of sitting (kneeling has almost disappeared) in a circle or semi-circle round the altar, with the priest facing the people, brings everyone closer together, but it also closes off the space. These arrangements are inhibiting for the half-believer, the newcomer, the casual visitor or someone who wants to be private. Such worship does not make it easy for the outsider to participate, but is for a self-contained group.

Furthermore, the emphasis on the Church as the Lord's family is an unfortunate image – our experience of "families" is decidedly ambiguous, and there are many people who have little or no family. Yet "family" occurs five times in the service called "The Baptism of Children". The children are to be brought up as Christians "within the family of the Church"; as they grow up they need the encouragement "of the family". When the child is baptized, the priest says, "You become a member of a new family – where all Christian people will be your brothers and sisters". A prayer is offered to God asking that He will receive the child into the "family of your Church". And after the Baptism, the priest says, "We welcome you into the Lord's family". This emphasis on the Church as a family reinforces the exclusive way in which it is perceived.[1]

The new Funeral Service also fails to recognize the considerable number of people whose sense of membership is cloudy and vague, and yet who, when it comes to critical moments, wish to belong. At the funeral of a young man who died of AIDS, I had to decide which funeral service to use. Neither he nor his partner were Christians, though they were not atheists or agnostics. Nevertheless, his friends and family wanted a religious service. I felt that it would have been quite wrong to use the new Funeral Service in view of its complexity. For instance, at one point the second part of the Te Deum is read:

> You Christ are the King of Glory
> The eternal Son of the Father.
> When you became man to set us free:
> You did not abhor the Virgin's womb.
> You overcame the sting of death
> And opened the Kingdom of the earth to all believers.
> You are seated at God's right hand in glory.
> We believe that you will come and be our judge.
> Come then Lord and help your people
> bought with the price of your own blood
> And bring us with your saints
> to glory everlasting.

A commentary published by the Liturgical Commission of the Church of England says about these words: "This is entirely appropriate at this point. It is in the nature of a congregational acclamation . . . and it picks up the theme of the Christian hope that 'The Lord will bring us with your saints to glory everlasting'."

But in spite of the modernization of the words the text is dense, and to anyone unfamiliar with Christian doctrine perhaps incomprehensible. In twelve lines there are references to the Incarnation, the Virgin Birth, the Resurrection, the Ascension, the Day of Judgement, the Sacrifice on the Cross, and the hope of heaven. To have confronted that congregation head on with these confident assertions of praise and hope would have generated dismay and anger.

The other serious criticism is the language of the new services. The language is explicit, clear, precise and direct. But it is also didactic in style; the Alternative Service Book is full of reminders and instructions. We are told quite clearly what we are to do. Thus, the introduction to morning and evening prayer:

> We have come together as the family of God
> in our Father's presence
> to offer him praise and thanksgiving,
> to hear and receive His Holy word,
> to bring before Him the needs of the world,
> to ask His forgiveness of our sins,
> and to seek His grace,
> that through His Son Jesus Christ
> we may give ourselves to His service.

Contrast this with the introduction to morning and evening prayer in the Prayer Book:

> Dearly beloved brethren, the Scripture moveth us in sundry places to acknowledge and confess our manifold sins and wickedness; and that we should not dissemble nor cloke them before the face of Almighty God our heavenly Father; but confess them with an humble, lowly, penitent, and obedient heart; to the end that we may obtain forgiveness of the same, by his infinite goodness and mercy.

The use of two words where one will do ("acknowledge and confess", "manifold sins and wickedness", "dissemble nor cloke"), and the rhythm of the sentences, include and invite the listeners to participate; they are not being bombarded with instructions.

Again, the introduction to the greeting Kiss of Peace is typical of the bald, clear style of the Alternative Service Book.

> We are the Body of Christ.
> In the one Spirit we were all baptized into one body.
> Let us then pursue all that makes for peace
> and builds up our common life.

The Body of Christ is a powerful, packed image. St Paul used the phrase to convey, almost literally, how the Church and all its members was, in essence, the resurrected body of Jesus Christ. It is not in its original sense a metaphor or a symbol, but a direct statement of an extraordinary fact. But the very directness of its use here leaves little to the imagination; it is also coded language, only for those "in the know".

The new sentence is typical of the classroom feel of the Alternative Service Book. We are being told something:

> In the one Spirit we were all baptized into one body.

Then follows a vague exhortation. Does it point to ourselves as individuals, to the Church, to the whole world?

> Let us then pursue all that makes for peace, and builds up our common life.

What has happened is that the Alternative Service Book fails to relate to anything beyond itself. It does not engage with living. There is no resonance: our deepest aspirations and needs, our doubts and questionings, our anguish and our premonitions of glory, our times of trust and hope, are all bypassed. The language reflects a contraction of all the complexities and paradoxes of experience, and of religious experience, to the in-group, the "family" of the Church. The Kingdom of God hardly figures. It is as if God barely existed outside the club.

The Alternative Service Book is not another Book of Common Prayer. It is a church book, a manual for Christian congregations. Its self-confident assertions may make those who use it feel comfortable, but ultimately the language of the services leads to such a distancing from living that Christian faith seems not to relate to anything. And that is the sad irony of the whole enterprise. A book which sets out to make worship more intelligible and up to date ends up being banal and irrelevant.

It is easy enough to criticize. And the inadequacies of rites, rituals and ceremonies appear, after constant use, and cannot always be foreseen. But in the face of the severity of these criticisms about the Alternative Service Book, any reforms will have to be more than a tinkering about with the language. They must start from a consideration of the fundamental impulse behind worship. And that is Celebration.

Celebration is expressed in adoration, praise and thanksgiving for God's universe, and for God's creation which has been entrusted to us for our pleasure and enjoyment.

Today worship and pleasure may appear to have little in common. That is because our rituals and church services domesticate, imprison and tame the wildness and beauty of God, and also because our understanding of enjoyment is so debased. Nowadays it is suspect because it interferes with productivity and work; celebrations are, strictly speaking, useless. Pleasure is merely another commodity to be earned, bought and spent, and the more expensive and luxurious the pleasure is, the better it is.

But pleasure in a truly Christian perspective is less about consuming and more about savouring, delighting in the world, recognizing that in everything there is something of God.

To take pleasure in this universe, and to express this in worship, is to show our relish, love and respect for the earth.

To take pleasure in God's creation means to express delight in the sensual and erotic. Eroticism usually means sexual sensation and gratification. It is thus cut off from the intensity of feelings which in loving relationships (well beyond sexual ones) becomes its true meaning. This is the intensity of feelings of self-worth, and of being valued, of our interdependence, of nothingness and pain, of tenderness and of anger, of our amazing capacity to create change, and of the possibilities of intimacy.

Passionate people get clobbered. Institutional religion often breeds a type of person whose full capacities for living, loving, struggling, laughing and dying are denied, so that he or she becomes acceptable. There is a deadness, a passionless quality about some expressions of Christianity – those which place on a pedestal the inaccessible Logos, the Word of God, whose pallid, virgin Son was born painlessly to a Virgin. (Instead, such Christians project their passion, which they try hard to ignore, on to women – whom they label whores, lesbians – and homosexuals, whom they insult as dykes, or faggots or poofs, and whose sole concern they believe is to lure and seduce and destroy anything that is good.)

Eroticism, as I have described it, should have a central place in the celebration and rituals of the Church. It means a proper respect and care for the body. If our bodies are merely prisons in which the spirit lives, then there is every reason to despise sexual feelings, and not bother about our own bodies or those of others. Faith becomes disfigured and disembodied – for there is then no understanding of God being God incarnate in flesh and blood, touch, smell and taste.

Respect and love for the body entails responsibility for it – diet, fasting, abstinence and exercise are part of this responsibility. And in worship (as in life) the ways in which we breathe, sit, stand, move, kneel, speak or sing, cannot be taken for granted. Such simple and essential human activities have to be taken seriously, but not self-consciously! This is a little of what I mean by expressing a proper delight in the sensual and erotic, as well as releasing our individual and corporate powers to imagine and to create. In this way celebration starts to reflect, to express delight and joy in all creation.

Worship which arises out of this celebration of God's universe (some four million years old) also recognizes the interdependence of everything – not just for one another, but of the earth and air, water and fire – the elements which we all share. Mystics and some scientists recognize our interdependence; they sense it as a vibrant example of God's grace. Without it we could not live, and the human task is to work with it, respect it and befriend it. Nowhere in our modern service books is there any acknowledgement of this extraordinary grace which sustains our planet.

A sense of interdependence inevitably fosters respect and tolerance, for when one person suffers, the rest suffer, and there can be no salvation for one person until the whole of creation is healed and transformed. When thanksgiving is offered for the wonder of creation in all its richness and diversity, then there is true worship. An obvious expression of this is the celebration of the multi-faith, multi-racial society which Britain has now become: nowhere in our service books is there any acknowledgement of this marvellous diversity.

And, after all, there is no such thing as a Hindu sky, or a Catholic moon or a Church of England sun. The mysterious forces which create the tide are the same on the Pacific as in North America.

The sacraments are the means through which this extravagant praise and thanksgiving for creation are offered; the pity is that the rites of the Church have so formalized and trivialized them.

Sacraments have their origins in bodily, messy and very human experiences – in dying and giving birth in Baptism, in eating and drinking together in Holy Communion, in calling out leaders in Ordination, in forgiving one another in penance or marriage, and in rubbing oil on bodies in Unction. In the words of the Catechism of the Prayer Book, they are "outward and visible signs of an inward and spiritual grace". These signs – water, bread, wine, oil, and the laying on of hands – are reminders of God's presence, sustaining and renewing the whole creation; they are signs of the love of God. Yet the primary sacrament to which all the sacraments point is the universe itself, and those bits of it of which we are most conscious – the planet and ourselves.

But that is not all – Christian worship is not a cosmic bath where the participants wallow in fantasies of love, beauty and harmony. The sacramental sense of creation invites a response; God is dependent on us, for creation has been entrusted to us. There is no holy, private, special realm over against life. It is *our* hands which are used for healing; *our* presence which stands with the outcast; *our* imagination and skill which helps the deserts to flower. The sacraments are reminders of this awesome responsibility. But we have fallen very short on living up to them. We can no longer take the earth for granted because we are slowly witnessing the progressive destruction of the natural world: the planet is being poisoned and ruined through the pollution of the air, the water and the soil. Celebration has both to nurture ways of showing respect for creation and also to enlarge the notion of sin and confession beyond personal peccadilloes. For over two thousand years intricate theological systems have been constructed about the nature, meaning and purpose of the sacraments, particularly the Holy Communion; but these systems have lost sight of this fundamental apprehension of the goodness of creation – all that there is is a sign of God's original and continuing blessing.

Yet the symbols of the sacraments – water and bread, for example – are themselves in jeopardy. If water has become so poisoned that it kills then how can it be a sign of regeneration and life? If the bread and wine are broken and shared for a few, how can that be in any sense a valid celebration, when there are one thousand million people who are regularly hungry – unless those who celebrate it challenge a political and economic system which enslaves great numbers of people and destroys the earth?

Worship expresses praise to God through Jesus, because Jesus disclosed the reality of the Kingdom of God. Thus praise should have an edge to it. Praise should establish who is who. Those who praise God say, "Our loyalty, our trust are given unreservedly to Jesus Christ and the Kingdom, and not to anybody or anything else. The Kingdom has first and complete claim on our lives. Absolutely nothing else is worthy of receiving unqualified assent."

Yet this is not the impression we gain from the sight of large, resolutely cheerful congregations on television's "Songs of Praise". All too often worship in Britain reveals a Church that is too settled, too at home in the world. For praise to be praise, there would be a vivid sense of a community in exile in a strange land, struggling and pressing forward.

Above everything else, Christians celebrate the Resurrection of Jesus as a past event, but also as a present experience opening out into the future. The experience is one of freedom and hope. Easter celebrates the freedom from death, and therefore from the power of death over life – whether it is death in the literal sense, or the economic death which allows millions to starve, or the silent death of the cynical and despairing soul.

It is a festival of laughter, and a mockery of the pretensions and cruelties of the mighty and powerful. It is also a festival of hope, because the ministry of Jesus was and is validated; it is a festival which has therefore a passionate utopian quality. It does not indulge in fantasies, but promotes a vision of what the world could and should be – informed by the stories and experiences of the Jewish and Christian traditions where the promises of God's Kingdom have been revealed. The Celebration articulates and anticipates this new creation of order, unity, harmony and justice.[2]

How are these Easter "experiences" to be celebrated? How can a radical sacramental delight and pleasure in creation find expression in worship?

It is the artist – the painter, the poet, the composer, the musician, the sculptor, the dancer, and the creative "artist" in each of us – who could help the Church to embody these insights of grace.

The artist is central and crucial to the matter of celebration. Artists are the teachers and educators of the spirit; they cut through pretensions; they call attention to our humanity – the life we have somehow forfeited and our longing for the restoration of paradise. The artist teaches us to feel, and brings us to our knees; there religion and art meet; there the imagination changes, restores and enlarges our hopes and visions.

So long have the artists gone from our churches that we hardly know what to do or how to receive them. Yet their presence is invaluable. Some will work alone; other collaboratively. Some relate readily to Christian symbols; others find their inspiration elsewhere. No matter – their spirit is energizing and renewing, and their indestructible if fragile gifts (in all of us and not just in professionals) have to be honoured and respected.

In 1985 two artists-in-residence – sculptors – worked at St James's Church, Piccadilly. Together with children from local schools, visitors to the church, all manner of people, they created a great serpent. On a chill, damp, February afternoon it proceeded with ceremony and solemnity through London, a sublime

symbol of what the arts should be about – provocative, beautiful, moving, jocular, showstopping. (The police, fearing a riot,
were there in large numbers. But all they had to do was to halt
the traffic at Piccadilly Circus.) The link between "religion" and
"the world" was made so clearly: the serpent was a fragile
framework of beauty and care, blown by the wind, small against
the powers of the world. It was the work of many hands; the
blazing eyes and tongue (the little generator actually worked),
the lights flashing on and off on the body, the legs carrying and
accompanying it – past Whitehall, across the Thames, down to
the Festival Hall, all worked together to make a modest, but
sublime symbol.

Celebration takes many forms and is expressed in differing
styles;[3] Christian communities which begin to discover the
possibilities of celebration soon find they are developing a local
style, like regional accents. There is no reason why there should
be a universal style. Nothing is more depressing than for a
church to try to ape the cathedral style of worship, when its
members do not possess those particular talents. Celebration
takes many different forms; there will be times when solemnity,
formality and austerity are called for, times for silence, times for
the expression of corporate powerlessness and lament, times for
gratitude for renewed energy, times of penitence, times of shared
intimacy and simplicity, times of extravagance when no energy
or expense is spared.[4]

These intimations of some of the factors in Christian celebration (and there are many others) are a long way from the
experience of church services noted at the start of the chapter.
What is to be done? It is not a question of rearranging this or
that, or including something to "brighten the service"; rather it
is putting the Kingdom of God in a central position and
recovering the conviction of God's original blessing in creation.
As this happens, so the celebration will inevitably change, and
as the celebration in turn begins to nourish the Kingdom
community, so the priorities of Christians will change to such a
degree that a Reformation of the Church becomes inescapable.
And it is to this, finally, that we turn.

Reformation

Jesus lived and died for the Kingdom of God. It was his passion, his life. Nothing else mattered. If the Kingdom of God becomes the passion and life of the Church, so that nothing else matters, we shall experience a Reformation, the like of which has never been seen. It will be a Reformation in the practice of the Church, in the thinking of the Church, and in the shape of the Church.

A. THE PRACTICE

The Reformation should bring an end to ecclesiastical games. One such game being played in the Church of England (and in all the main-line churches) is the battle between Liberals and Traditionalists. The issue is coming to a head over the ordination of women, but that is only the tip of a vast iceberg. The other issues are belief in the Virgin Birth, and belief in the Resurrection of Jesus Christ, with both being related to the nature of the person of Jesus. The Traditionalists affirm that what they believe is what is taught by the Creeds to which Christians are required to assent; they assert the authority of the Bible. They accuse the Liberals of accommodating the beliefs of the Church to their own experience, and in effect of making up Christianity as they go along; they accuse the Liberals of betraying the Christian faith, and say that they should either come to their senses or leave the Church.

This is a game, even if it is a game which is taken with great seriousness, and in which some people have been and will be hurt. It is a game because the centrality of the Kingdom of God has been lost. After all, beyond a certain point the arguments give out; they run into the sand. These intellectual gymnastics take place in a weary, depressed Church – while beyond it there is the desolate, bleak and violent landscape of millions of people starving, and here, in our own country, the growing numbers of the poor. How, in God's name, can these arguments dominate the energy and time of Christian people in such conditions? What has happened to the compassion, which we saw was the hallmark of the life of Jesus, of those who make these matters a top priority and concern of the Church?

Jesus was not interested in matters of corrrect or incorrect belief. He did not see the truth as that which had to be "upheld" or "maintained". For him all that mattered was what a person actually does. The search of Jesus was for true practice – orthopraxis – and not true doctrine – orthodoxy. When all has been said, and said again, faith is not a way of just speaking or just thinking, but a way of living. Actions speak louder than words.[1]

In the magnificent, sombre set piece of the story of the Last Judgement (Matthew 25:31–46) this is made painfully clear. It is the only detailed description of the Last Judgement in the gospels. Already the religious and political authorities are closing in on Jesus; they want him removed. It is the last story Jesus tells before his passion, and it is a summary of all his teaching. The scene is the heavenly court where the world is gathered before the Son of Man on judgement day; strange as it is to us, that picture would have been only too familiar to Jesus's audience, and to the Christian communities for which Matthew wrote. They believed that God's judgement was imminent. Moreover, this was not just the picture of the judgement heralding the end of the world, but also a picture of the judgement which was operating in the present at every moment. The awesome picture of the Son of Man as Judge is offset by the ordinary events which Jesus took to make his point: in Palestine at nightfall it was customary for a shepherd to divide his flocks – the goats preferred shelter, the sheep the open air.

The inheritors of the Kingdom are those who fed the hungry, gave water from their precious water bottles to the thirsty, welcomed the stranger, gave clothing to protect the naked from the searing heat of the day and the bitter cold at night, comforted the sick, and visited those in prison. The significance of anyone's life is judged by the compassion they showed; those who showed none were punished, "Depart from me, ye cursed, into everlasting fire".

There is nothing particularly special about that part of the story; but what is astonishing is the statement that "Inasmuch as ye have done it unto one of the least of my brethren, ye have done it unto me". That is to say that in the faces of the hungry, the thirsty, the stranger, the naked, the sick and the prisoner, is the face of God; and that they are, at one and the same time, "the King", the "Son of Man who shall come in his glory, the Judge" (v. 31). In other words, it is the poor and the oppressed who stand in judgement on the rest of us. If the Gospel is not good news for the poor (and that they alone can say), then the Church is judged by the poor. The exploited Third World stands in judgement on America and the rich European nations. In Britain there are those who blame the decline and decay of our society on the workshy unemployed, the black kids who are just layabouts, and the greedy Trade Unions.[2]

Judgement in the story of sheep and goats and everywhere else in the gospels is different. The dole queues are the judgement on the rest of us. It is an upside-down judgement. The angry, bitter and vulnerable eyes of those who have been excluded from what the rest of us enjoy are the eyes of God, who shares the anguish, pain and protest.

Thus the story says that to support the poor, God is glorified, and when the poor are ignored and rejected, God is ignored and rejected. Furthermore, the "righteous" ones make no claim to be good; they are surprised to learn that they had in fact been loving God, in feeding those who were hungry. What they did was done without any thought of reward.

The words "righteous" and "unrighteous" are more accurately translated as "just" and "unjust". The most important biblical aspect of justice is that justice happens when what has been taken away is justly restored. In other words, it is those who are responsible for the persistence of poverty – those who get rich at the expense of others – who are the unjust, the oppressors.

It is not individuals who are gathered together before God, but the nations of the world, and they are on trial. The questions about the hungry, the poor, the stranger, the sick are directed to the nations, and thus to those to whom the formation of public policy is entrusted.

These questions are raised directly from the text, and they are distinctly uncomfortable. When I preach about this story, congregations often feel battered, even personally assaulted, and many react defensively. "What can we do about it?", they say. "You just make us feel guilty – we can't help who we are." Some say that the sermon was too political. The preacher will experience resentment and anger, but it is misplaced anger because it is the biblical text itself which is giving everyone a bad time – and that includes the preacher. None of us are left off the hook.

It has to be said at once that the poor are just as cruel and selfish as the rest of the human race. However, that is not the point. The fact of their poverty is the fact of God's judgement – their presence, their cries, their aspirations are revelatory, disclosing that judgement.

Thus the fundamental issue for the health of Christianity is the extent to which the poor find the Gospel true and liberating. And since they are largely indifferent to it, there is something diseased about our churches.

The reasons for this indifference and the failure of the churches to establish anything but a fragile presence in our inner cities have been well documented in *Faith in the City* (the Report of the Archbishop of Canterbury's Commission on Urban Priority Areas). The recommendations to the Church are about ways of strengthening and enabling local Christian communities to grow in urban priority areas. For those to be implemented, there will need to be not only more funds available, but also resources of people, with all their skills and imagination.

None of this will happen unless the power base of the Church – suburban and middle-class – shifts, so that a real partnership between the Church of the poor and the rest of the Church comes into being. This means, for example, a deliberate attempt to ensure that the voice of the inner city church – white AND black – is much more than a token voice in the Synod and Councils of the Church. It means that there needs to be positive discrimination in the deployment of clergy and other paid workers in the direction of inner cities — and away from the flourishing suburban churches.

It means too that everything that can be done has to be done to establish the Church as a more credible institution in the eyes of the poor, so that it can speak with them and for them. But this will only happen if the priorities of the Kingdom of God become an overriding preoccupation of the churches — and even then it will certainly be a bumpy ride, for no one relinquishes power and influence readily.

The recommendations in *Faith in the City* are for the Church of England, and particularly for those who are active, influential and powerful in the Councils of the Church. Its appeal is therefore limited. What can the rest of us do?

There is an obvious need for getting wise about attitudes to poverty and the poor, because many are prejudiced, wrong and immoral. There are some, for example, who even deny the existence of poverty, and who hold to a completely false opinion that "things are getting generally better for everyone". There are others who *blame* the poor: they are poor because they are lazy; they deserve everything they get. They are the "scroungers" and "scum". The solution for the poor — on this analysis, if it can be called that — is to make life so unbearable that they will do everything they can to change their situation. But this cruel policy has never ever worked. The poor become patronized and persecuted. Others explain the facts of poverty in terms of a cycle of deprivation or the "culture" of poverty: here the solution is to "help" individuals out of the poverty trap by building up their self-confidence. None of these solutions work; the poor exist because circumstances beyond their control have created their situation. The persistence of poverty is due to the new factor of de-industrialization and the collapse of our manufacturing base. Any analysis has to address a whole series of questions about what makes for human fulfilment. If there is no prospect of work for some, what is needed to live a fulfilled life? These questions are about the nature and future of our society. And it is the poor themselves who are not only the bearers of God's judgement, but also our teachers; they set the pace.

In my exposition of the parable of the sheep and the goats, the preacher has the chance to bring the invisible powerless into the midst of the congregation. The preacher speaks through the hearts and eyes of the poor. But there are other ways in which the poor become the teachers.

Victorian Christianity was the impetus for a multitude of good works in our cities: the rich helped the poor. Now the roles need to be reversed. Churches in urban priority areas should create forums whereby the poor can speak of their experience to those who are privileged and powerful. Then some of the unlearning about the poor begins to happen. A striking but small example of this happened at St James's, Piccadilly, in the cold spell of February 1987; for ten days the church opened its doors for anyone to come and sleep and have something to eat. This event coincided with an appeal for the restoration of the church and the development of its programmes. I had been invited to meet several wealthy and influential people whom I hoped to persuade to support our work. At the end of dinner I invited them all to come to the church to meet our "guests" as we called them. They graciously refused, except for one person. He was intrigued by the idea of seeing some four hundred people bedding down in an elegant, baroque church. I introduced him to a 28-year-old man from Newcastle. He had not worked for five years, and his marriage had finally collapsed. He had heard that he might get a job in London, but he had been on the streets for six months and found nothing. As the conversation progressed, I noticed how the young man's confidence grew in the telling of his story, and how the rich man became steadily more uneasy. He was touched by the young man's plight, but did not know what could be done. Some days later, the rich man asked to see me. He was troubled by what had happened to him in the church that night. And then he said, "I have always thought of myself as a free person, and in a limited way I am, but I realized later that I was part of the very system which had made Michael (that was the young man's name) poor. And even though I am wealthy, I felt quite powerless." That was the start of that person's liberation. Slowly but surely he is making changes in his own life style – he is living more simply, but he is also trying to see how his extensive resources can be used for the poor. He is having to make considerable adjustments in his life.

There are, of course, those who say that the poor will have to wait . . . until this or that remedy is proposed.

Adrian Smith, a Catholic monk and theologian, has worked in inner-city Liverpool for fifteen years. In *Passion for the Inner City*, he writes of the poor:

> They wait for the dole; they wait for the hint of employment; they wait for supplementary benefit; they wait for a sector of society to really live up to the philosophy of equal opportunities; they wait for the bureaucratic system to check its files; they wait for a white racist society to admit its own spiritual paralysis which prevents its facing up to itself with honesty . . . A society which forces people to wait . . . is a society which has chosen the path of the oppressor.

These are the poor – the unemployed, the long-term unemployed, the single-parent family, over 50 per cent of whom are on Supplementary Benefit, the single homeless, the elderly surviving on their old age pension, the large family dependent on a low-paid worker or on Supplementary Benefit. They are our neighbours. Nothing I have said about compassion – about our interconnection, our interdependence – makes any sense unless the issue of poverty is central to our concerns. If all men and women are created in the image of God, and valued for the unique, graceful person that each can be, and if there are some whom we choose not to value, then there is injustice, and the web of interdependence is shattered.

And then in the practice of the Church, the prophets are to be guarded and offered sanctuary. The Church guards the prophets, and offers them friendship and sanctuary. There are well known prophetic figures – Martin Luther King, Dorothy Day, Bishop Trevor Huddleston and Archbishop Desmond Tutu. But there are also many others who reveal something of the divine radiance in their passion for justice and peace, in their care and love for the poor. In our own day, these prophetic figures and communities often witness outside the Christian Church. The women at Greenham Common are typical.

Prophets and prophetic communities are not stern and strident. They are only too conscious that they are part of the mess. They have generous hearts, and when their warnings are done they weep with those who weep. Denunciation is always balanced by lamentation in the prophetic tradition. The prophets speak of endings – of how the familiar, acceptable and accepted ways of doing things no longer work, for no one knows anything any more. The powerful wish for no change – "as it was in the beginning is now and ever shall be"; they see no alternative future. Sometimes where there is little to be done, there is only the sighing and the sorrowing – in their poetry bringing to public expression the grief and anguish of those who suffer, and mourning on behalf of those who do not yet see the end. Jeremiah's poetry is the most telling example of this in the Old Testament; and in the gospels, the weeping of Jesus is decisive – weeping over Lazarus, over Jerusalem. For the powerful man or woman machismo is everything – but not for Jesus Christ.

Prophets are not politicians – they don't have programmes. A prophet is like the artist; she invites us to feel again. Her witness provides vitality, energy and the gift of refreshing, and new images for us to draw on. She is a poet of the spirit and disturber of the peace. The horizon we are invited to step out towards is the Kingdom of God.

Prophets are never popular in churches (or anywhere else for that matter). They are seen as a nuisance. But a church passionate about the Kingdom will, with the prophet, warn, watch and wait and keep the Vigil, make lament, provide sanctuary – classic expressions of a Church, a Christian presence, resisting inhumanity and the heavy hand of injustice.[3]

B. THOUGHT

A Reformation in practice has to be informed and sustained by a Reformation in thought. As the Church becomes more "politicized", drawn deeper and deeper into public affairs and into all the problems, disturbances and dangers we face, so connections and conscious interactions between what is believed and what is done have to be made and re-made. By "Church" I mean primarily those men and women who are serious about their vocation as servants of the Kingdom and working that out in their own lives; but I also mean reports of church agencies on political, economic or social questions, and statements by Church leaders. Those connections and interactions can only be made if people know what they are talking about. Questions of expertise and competence cannot be avoided. At the end of a detailed analysis of the role of the Church of England in *Politics Today*, the editor, George Moyser, writes,

> Until the Church is more intellectually serious about its involvement in politics, and tries to link its political and social ethics into a more developed theological understanding of man as a political animal, its claims to be taken seriously in politics will founder.

There are other interactions which need to be strengthened and developed: I have touched on five areas – the Jewish roots of Christianity, the mystical tradition, the artist, feminism and the presence of other religions. Here the questions arise as to what should be assimilated into the teachings and traditions of Christianity, and what should be discarded. To consider these questions competently entails first-hand experience, intellectual competence and discernment. And unless there is some coherent basis out of which this meaning of connections takes place, the result is confusion and chaos. It would be natural to turn to theologians for help. But as far as Western Christianity is concerned, they cannot help – for they are in the wrong place.

Some years ago I was responsible for running in-service training programmes for clergy from inner-city areas; the purpose of the programme was to offer support and encouragement in their work by helping them make sense of their lives and ministry, and thus enable them to establish priorities. It was clear that part of the process of "making sense" was a theological one: how could their faith provide a framework for what they did?

We felt inadequate; from among ourselves it seemed that we

could not provide the answers. So I went to see a Professor of Theology at a well known university. I told him my problem. I explained to him the conditions under which the clergy worked, their isolation, their lack of success, the uncertainty about their role, the social problems landing day after day on their doorsteps. "What", I asked, "does theology have to offer those brave inner-city priests?" He paused, looked at me, looked out of the window, and said, "That's a very good question". That was all he could say.

Where has theology been done? St Paul did theology everywhere – on the road, at sea, in prison, in synagogues. But after Paul, and with the expansion of the early Church, the doing of theology was restricted to certain places. First it was associated with the "seat" of the Bishop, for the Bishop sat to instruct the clergy and people in matters of Christian doctrine. Later, theologians were found in the monasteries. After the Reformation, the Roman Catholic Church studied and taught theology at seminaries; in the Church of England it happened at the ancient universities of Oxford, Cambridge and Durham (and then at others).

Theology was done by men in privileged positions. Because the setting has been academic, the area of discourse has been narrow and specialized. Hence much theology has been inaccessible, certainly to some clergy, and to most men and women. Theology has operated on a "development trickle-down model"; theologians pass down their work to the clergy, some of whom digest it, and pass it on to the people in the pews. The result is a thoroughly inarticulate, ill-educated church, with the learning and the knowledge left in the hands of a few. Thus many Christian people are effectively intellectually disabled and impoverished – whether they are "educated" or not.

Most theologians are not in a position to help this process of interaction and the making of connections. They are hard pressed in working for universities which pay their salaries, and the pressure on them is to produce academic specialist work of such a quality that it will ensure the good standing of their department.

Most bishops and church leaders are too busy, preoccupied with pastoral and administrative matters. And, given the way that theology has been done, it is inevitable that most clergy and laity are incompetent.

Of course there are exceptions – among individual theologians, church leaders, clergy and men and women. But university departments of theology are being cut back, and Christianity in Britain has a rapidly declining intellectual base from which any necessary thinking and reflection can take place. This is dangerous, because superstition and bigotry thrive when the churches stop thinking; and intellectual exploration is regarded with fear and suspicion – in case "the simple faith of ordinary people is undermined". So theologians today are generally mistrusted, particularly among those who never read them.

Therefore, theology has to be liberated; theologians need to be freed from the captivity of their studies. They must be ready to be relocated, to move to another place – to do theology on the streets.

Given the impasse into which the intellectual, thinking life of Christianity has fallen, leaving a vacuum, there is only one thing to do, and that is to start the process of making connections from the experience of men and women. In other words, the beginnings of reflection and understanding are in experience (and not in the contemplation or the rearranging of metaphysical truths).

The process of street theology begins with the old Socratic maxim of "An unexamined life is not worth living".

In one of his diaries, Che Guevara writes about how he was accused of being a revolutionary. His enemies said that his soldiers went to the villages, raped the women, shot the men and burnt down the houses. Che said that what in fact he did was to gather the people together, and invite them to tell the story of their lives – and that was the Revolution. The telling of the story led the peasants to understand their own predicament – what was going on in their society and why!

Sometimes this analysis needs the help of experts for the purpose of clarification, and sociologists or political theorists may be called in. Illuminating this process is the Christian experience – both of the past and of the present.

It is a method anyone can use, because the basic form of it is the story. The Bible is mostly a story book, Jesus spoke about the Kingdom of God in stories, and past Christian experience is best understood as a story.

Stories are not generally trusted as a way of knowing, but for anyone coming to Christianity either for the first time or fresh after an absence, the story is the foundation out of which all knowledge comes. For too long Christianity has been addicted to an abstract, conceptual and systematic approach which effectively separates thinking from living, believing from doing. This is not to decry, for example, the creeds, which represent the consensus of the Christian community at certain times, and certain echoes of ferocious debates and quarrels which still engage Christians (on the person of Christ, for example). But the creeds, like much theology, are secondary; because they are reflections on the story.

The primal story in the Old Testament is that of the deliverance of Israel from slavery to freedom, of God leading Israel in the wilderness to the good land which God had provided. In the New Testament, the primal story is that the New Age of the Kingdom has been inaugurated by the Coming of Christ – in his life, death, burial, resurrection and exaltation, and the outpouring of the Spirit. Much of the biblical literature expands on these stories, adds to them, reflects on them as the communities become settled, and then offers theological reflections.

These stories need to be owned and appropriated – to be told, and shared and retold and passed on; they become part of the lifeblood of every member of the community. Thus they inform, determine, encourage and legitimate action; it is not a question of trying to make the stories relevant. There has to be that same process of "passing over" which I said was essential for attentive listening to other faiths (page 69). It is allowing them to seep into our consciousness – in all their strangeness. In an intellectually barren situation such as British Christianity is experiencing, the only way forward is to start all over again – and that is

95

simply to possess the Christian story, or that part of it which resonates with our experience.

It is a matter of making connections – from the Bible and the tradition to our own situation in Britain. Yet that is not all. The understanding of the situation – of our situation in Britain – is what is happening in the area where I work, to my neighbourhood, to my family and to myself? And after all the analysis is over, our own lives – personal and public – are stories. But that is difficult to grasp. It is not easy to move from a perception of life as just "one damn thing after another" to that of a story which has a shape, a form and movement to it. It is even more difficult to interpret this story of an individual or a Christian community as bearing itself the marks of a sacred text, so that there God is seen disclosing His goodness and luring His people on into further tasks for the Kingdom.

We need to find urgently from within or beyond the churches people who can help this process to happen; theologians and scholars have their place, but a limited one. They can at least provide background information. Some may have gifts in making the Jewish/Christian experience of three thousand years available; others will help us to own and use the language of faith so that we are no longer mystified and disabled.[4]

The telling of these stories can happen when the community gathers for worship. And if the making of connections seems so difficult, it can also become a most natural process. At St James's, Piccadilly during the Liturgy it is customary at the time for Notices not only for information about events and activities to be mentioned but also for anyone to share an experience which would be appropriate for such a gathering. Thus it is we hear stories of celebration, of anguish, of hopes dashed and rekindled, of anger and frustration at some cruelty in the world. We have heard stories of the courage of Christian communities in such different places as Nicaragua, the Soviet Union, South Africa – some of these stories are inspirational, and the gathering is invited to pass them on to others. Sometimes the stories are told in such a way that we want to know more, so that we can support them with money and time. Very often the stories make us thoughtful about our own actions, aware of our silence and collusion with wickedness. When the stories are told simply and directly in the context of the Liturgy, their power is immense.

It is natural for those who have not been trained as preachers to speak directly in stories. Some months after St James's Church was opened for homeless people to sleep in, I invited three members of our community actively involved in that event to preach the sermon reflecting on their experience. At first they found the task very difficult. Because they had experienced so many sermons which were mostly potted doctrine or easy exegesis of texts, which were then made "relevant", they began by trying to make intellectual statements about God's attitude to the rich and to the poor. In the preparation for the sermon I encourage them to forget whatever it was they thought they ought to say, and to start sharing their experience. Thus they told their stories – of what they did in those days, what they learnt, how helpless they felt, how important it was to keep on keeping on with these issues. As the stories were mulled over, so I offered some theological pointers to their experience, but in the event the stories were refined and told in such a way that they contained the meaning in themselves.

Radical Christianity of the sort I am describing is properly conservative. One of the most pressing problems for churches is that of their identity; as they are, churches are too much at home in our society. The way a Christian thinks and feels is determined more by her class, education and background, than by membership of her local church: the way she thinks and feels is part of the generally accepted culture. Her identity as a Christian has almost disappeared.

Thus many of us suffer from a collective amnesia, forgetting our roots and unable to acknowledge our history. So much is organized for amnesia, and against history. Memory is depreciated, and genuine hope is ridiculed, because a consumer, materialistic society says that everything has to be organized for now, for this moment.

This is understandable – when it is perceived that we are living in a Christian country with Christian values then there is no need to raise questions about identity; it can just be assumed.

But if the society is no longer Christian, and churches are not prepared to accommodate themselves so readily, then the powerful expression of the collective memories of Christian communities becomes inevitable, because they are conscious of being communities in exile.

Thus it is essential, as a genuine reforming movement begins to recover and reappropriate our collective memories in power and authenticity – stretching back three thousand years to the Exodus, looking at today and on into the future – for theologians to learn to mine these memories buried so deeply that they have almost been lost. It is better than all the striving after immediacy and relevance.

As this happens, so a new identity (but one which is in touch with the tradition) begins to emerge, and an alternative consciousness and practice is born.

It is here that the Bible is indispensable. The Bible is not an historical curiosity, or a textbook which provides "answers" or a book which proves this, that or the other. It is rather a collection of books which is a story of a covenant which God made with His people, a covenant which people made with each other, and a story of their relationship to the world. It is a book which contains memories which can be trusted, images which are powerful and dynamic; it is an account of a restless journey which calls the community who study it into new spheres of trust, and new directions of faithfulness in pursuit of a more humane future for the creation of God's Kingdom. Above everything else, the stories of the Bible are not just to be studied, directed, and then "left"; rather it is like a great ocean of stories, sayings and teachings which surge around us and invite us to plunge in, sometimes to linger in the depths before emerging with fresh and amazing perspectives. The Bible invites its readers to read and to listen, but we have also to be expected to be summoned and addressed.

There are, of course, some theologians and conservative Christians who will resist this approach. For them, it is a waste of time. They say that truth has been revealed (storytelling is altogether too subjective, too personal for them), and it has to be protected, proclaimed and applied to different situations.

It would be nice if this were so; part of our problem is that this notion of truth has been eroded, even ruined, by all those circumstances which I mentioned in the Introduction (page 14). But I believe truth has to be discovered in the doing of it – and the purpose of theology is to enlighten and inform actions.

Finally, there is a noble task to be undertaken, that of reclaiming, rebuilding and recreating the Christian framework of belief. But now is not the time for the grand design. Therefore for the time being, for this generation, we need to let the Christian story be – the story of the love and faithfulness of God in creation; of the breach between God and men and women; of God's initiative for reconciliation; of the expression of the goodness of God in Jesus; of the Resurrection and of the birth of the Church. Like the great classics of literature, this Christian story has a surplus of meanings. There is always more to be said; even when everything is explained, it is surrounded by a penumbra of mystery. So the liberals should not rush in to demolish it, reduce it, rationalize it, and make it relevant; and the conservatives should not be so strident in asserting that this, and this only, is the way and the case. Let the story be. Let us use what bits of it we can. One thing astronomy is telling us is just how little we know of God's universe. The mystery of God's creation of the Christian story is inexhaustible. If it is not all accessible, then let it be.

Instead we face up to all the ambiguities and complexities of our experience. In that story see God with us, desiring His goodness to be released. The task I have outlined is for the entire Christian community (and for anyone else!). It is an intellectual task; it calls for imagination. It is a journey of discovery and exploration. No questions are barred – everyone is listened to, particularly those on the margins. What a journey it could be!

C. THE SHAPE OF THE CHURCH

In the course of this book I have referred to the Church, the churches, the Church of England, the Anglican Communion and Christian churches. Although I write as an Anglican priest in the Church of England (and some of what I have written applies directly to the Church of England), my intention has been to blur denominational differences, because those who make the Kingdom of God a priority meet across denominations.

There is, however, one issue which will have to be addressed if Anglicans are to take a full part in this movement, and that is the role of the Anglican Communion as the established church.

I have spoken of the necessity to establish a Christian identity for the Church, and of the importance of its members' loyalty and allegiance to the Kingdom of God. Therefore, it is embarrassing that its chief pastors are appointed by the Queen on the advice of the Prime Minister, who herself receives recommendations from the Church. What is at stake here are questions of authority and identity. The Church in Synod should appoint its chief pastors, and if this means the end of the presence of the bishops in the House of Lords (the price which is paid for State interference), then so be it. It is odd that there is no outcry about this extraordinary procedure, let alone the secrecy with which it is carried out, and the lack of any public accountability. Perhaps it is that bishops do not figure in people's lives very much, in spite of sporadic interest by the media in bishops who "speak out". But there is another reason why this anomaly should be removed, and that is the particular circumstances in which this book has been written. In Britain today there is a steady erosion of liberal values. Respect for the individual, tolerance, restraint, collaboration, diversity, community – these words hardly describe the British "way of life". Liberals are blamed for the economic failure of the seventies, for forcing on the British public their élitist views about a multi-racial society, for removing the penal laws against homosexuality, and for liberalizing censorship.

The disappearance of "liberalism" has been replaced by an ugly authoritarianism; some political leaders, convinced of the absolute certainty of their convictions, cannot stand criticism and are scornful of anyone who criticizes.

Political leaders have power and influence. More than any other public figures they establish norms and legitimate fashion. Inevitably, this illiberalization spreads to other areas beyond the narrowly political. The Trade Unions, the BBC and the Press, the judiciary, civil servants, the universities, teachers – are all being brought into line.

The churches are being affected; the consistent hounding of the Archbishop of Canterbury in some quarters, abetted by much of the press, is caused by his determination to allow diversity, to welcome argument, the right to doubt and to disagree. The Archbishop's style of leadership is in keeping with that of many of his predecessors who held the ring, and who kept the Church of England together. Now he and some of his colleagues are regarded as dangerous and subversive and, it is said, the sooner they remove themselves the better it will be for church and nation.

Christian leadership is very different from the exercise of power as we experience it today. One of the astonishing facts of Jesus's life was its powerlessness. The events of Holy Week are reminders of Jesus as the Victim, the prisoner tortured and beaten, all privacy and belongings taken, and then crucified. But this was in keeping with the Jesus who washed the feet of his friends, and said, "He who would be great among you must be a servant. The last shall be first". And again, "Unless you become as little children you cannot enter the Kingdom of God".

How can a leader be powerless and still be a leader? How can he be weak, self-effacing, yet tough and still lead? How can a leader lead, yet bear witness to the love of God and absorb all the evil in the hearts of men and women? So accustomed are we to associating leadership with power that no satisfactory answers are available. Such a contradiction seems impossible to resolve.

But if the powerlessness of Jesus is a significant aspect of his life, then somehow the leadership of the Church has to reproduce this suitably for our own day and for the coming Reformation of Christianity. If some of the impulses and perceptions, attitudes and experiences of the many types of people I have written about in this book are to be part of this Reformation, then the way "powerless" leadership happens is crucial. In *Essays in Liberality*, Alec Vidler wrote:

101

A liberal-minded man is free from narrow prejudice, generous in his judgement of others, open-minded especially to
the reception of new ideas or proposals for reform. Liberal
is the opposite, not of conservatism but of fanatical or
bigoted or intransigent.

Perhaps in recovering this almost lost notion of this sort of
person we shall be discovering the style of a powerless leader
for our own day. And as the Church goes gladly towards the
margins of our society, these questions may be easier to answer.

At least it has to be said that to take seriously the powerless
leader means the end of clericalism, and clerical domination.
Historically, the priest is the paid professional who alone has
access to God: the clergy alone, through their professional
training, were authorized to preach and teach and administer.
This created a laity very dependent on the clergy.

Power over others (which is how the world perceives leadership, a view endorsed by the Church) has to give way to
empowering others. So, within any community, there will be a
mutual empowering of one another; the gifts of each person
are evoked and encouraged for the benefit of all. This is a long
way from the experience of hierarchical Christian churches
which are organized around the clergy as paid professionals.
(One of the issues which the end of clericalism raises is whether
the celebration of Baptism and Holy Communion, as well as
authorized teaching, should remain within the hands of the
clergy alone, something which causes much discussion and
disquiet.)

This way of thinking about leadership, which is so removed
from the realities in the world, means that the Church of
England must be free to choose its own pastors and must be
free of any political influences. It may be that if this were to
happen the Church would do no better, but that is not the
point – it must have the total freedom and authority to do
so, and particularly to attend to questions of the powerful
leader.

Again, the Church of England should have complete authority
over managing its affairs. It is a question of its identity. Now,

the Synod has only a delegated authority, and on important issues Parliament has the last word. A Kingdom Church would wish to see that the shape of its life was determined in its own councils under the guidance of the Spirit!

This means effectively the disestablishment of the Church of England, but this will only become an issue as the Church becomes less of an institution and more of a movement, so that its presence as a State church will become undesirable.

Vital to the growth of a movement is the nurture of its members. The journey I have indicated is hard; there is the inevitability of conflict, unpopularity and failure, as well as laughter and levity on the way. Therefore, people need to empower, encourage and strengthen one another, not just for its own sake, but for the sake of the Kingdom.

A Reformed Church will generate a variety of different forms of Christian community. There is absolutely nothing sacred about the pattern of church-going we know or know about — that is, of between a hundred and a hundred-and-fifty people gathered in a church building with a paid professional leading them. As the movement for the Kingdom spreads, so new style monasteries and convents, shared households, all sorts of networks of small cells, sustained by churches and cathedrals, will grow; a web of different combinations of people living, working, praying, struggling and celebrating together will be woven into the fabric of our society. The size of these groups, communities, churches, however they are defined, is determined to the extent its members are supported and encouraged. Invariably this means that many congregations are too large, unless there is a network of smaller units where people's gifts and talents and energies are mobilized.

There is no blueprint for this Reformation. The sole criterion is what we have been shown of the Kingdom of God revealed in Jesus Christ. After that, it has to be fashioned and refashioned, created and re-created in our own day in our own place.

There is no guarantee of success: there is plenty of evidence in history that institutional religion will do everything it can to marginalize the Kingdom. There is no reason to believe that the situation is any different today.

And Christians who long for the Church to become a movement for the Kingdom should not take themselves too seriously. We are only one of many voices clamouring for attention. Modesty, prudence and simplicity are as much part of our style as struggle and celebration.

Yet we should not be too despondent. There are signs of the coming of the Kingdom of God everywhere. I think of a rich man who gladly gives his wealth to the poor, and regards it as a privilege to do so. I think of a group of women – from Soweto in South Africa – whose friendship I cherish because their dignity, forbearance and laughter in the face of appalling provocation has enriched my life. I think of an Anglican priest in an inner-city parish, whose love for the people he lives among is matched only by his anger at the indifference of governments to their plight. I think of a woman in her late sixties who witnesses to another way of living at Greenham Common. I think of a nurse in a mental hospital who still, after many years, treats her patients with respect. I think of a good neighbour to many in her street. I think of an artist, fragile yet indestructible in his spirit, nourishing many human hearts. I think of those who, though weak and vulnerable, have grown generous hearts and bother about others.

These people are signs of the Kingdom. And if you would like to be part of such a company, then don't wait to set up a committee, just find someone who shares your interest. The Reformation is in your hands.

NOTES AND FURTHER READING

Oscar Wilde said, "The originality I mean which we ask from the artist is originality of treatment, not of subject. It is only the unimaginative who ever invent. The true artist is known by the use he makes of what he annexes, and he annexes everything." But that's the best excuse for plagiarism. The following bibliography is not complete; I only recommend books which have helped to shape each chapter.

INTRODUCTION

1. Robert Lifton's work on "psychic numbing" and "collective amnesia" prompted these words. See his *Survivors of Hiroshima* (New York, Random House, 1967), *History and Human Survival* (New York, Random House, 1961) and his anthology *In a Dark Time*, with Nicholas Humphrey (Macmillan).

2. *The Secularization of the European Mind in the Nineteenth Century*, a thorough and careful exposition of the complex process of secularization. Owen Chadwick (Cambridge University Press).

3. The best exposition of the idiocy of the Fundamentalist approach is James Barr's *Fundamentalism* (SCM).

4. "The Closeness of God". I have assumed this, and not argued the case. To have done this would have meant a different sort of book.

CHAPTER 1

1. I first read this story in Gerald Priestland's *The Case Against God*, chapter 1, "Case for the Prosecution" (Collins Fount), but, like the best stories, I have heard it told on several occasions.

2. There is a vast literature on the Holocaust. A useful survey is to be found in *The Minimal Self – Psychic survival in*

troubled times (chapter 3), Christopher Lasch (Picador);
also "The Holocaust as Interruption" (*Concilium* No. 175,
T. & T. Clark Ltd).
2. To be found in Elie Wiesel's *Night* (Penguin).
3. "The Night Sky of the Lord" – by Alan Ecclestone (Darton,
Longman & Todd).
4. In his massive books (like Bruckner's symphonies), *Jesus*
(Collins) and *Christ* (SCM Press) Edward Schillebeeckx.
writes inspiringly about the Kingdom. Also Albert Nolan's
Jesus before Christianity (SCM); and *God's Kingdom* by
George V. Pixley (SCM).
5. See *A Call to Conversion* by Jim Wallis (Lion Publishing).
The author brings out the fullness of the meaning of
conversion.

CHAPTER 2
1. *Becoming Adult, Becoming Christian* by James Fowler
(Harper & Row).

CHAPTER 3
1. *True God* by Kenneth Leech (SPCK), an exploration in
spiritual theology. See chapter 5, "God of the Desert", and
chapter 6, "God of Cloud and Darkness".
2. See the account of the correspondence between Rosemary
Reuther and Thomas Merton in *Merton – A Biography* by
Monica Furlong (Darton, Longman & Todd).

CHAPTER 4
1. See *Feminine in the Church*, Monica Furlong (SPCK) and
"Women – Invisible in Church and Theology", *Concilium*,
No. 85.
2. *In Memory of Her*, Elizabeth Schussler Fiorenza (SCM)
3. See *Women Ministers – how women are redefining
traditional roles*, Ed. Judith Weisdman (Harper & Row).

CHAPTER 5

1. This chapter draws heavily on *No Other Name*, Paul Knitter (SCM) – a comprehensive survey of attitudes of Christians to other faiths.

CHAPTER 6

1. *Original Blessing* by Matthew Fox (Bear & Co) is the most comprehensive and systematic account of this neglected theme.
2. See Jurgen Moltmann's *The Power of the Powerless* and in particular "Easter – the Festal Protest against Death", p. 122. (This book of sermons is the best introduction to Moltmann's theology.)
3. Two shining examples of new liturgies are the beautiful prayers, psalms and poems in *All desires known* by Janet Morley (published by the Movement for the Ordination of Women, Napier Hall, Hide Place, Vincent Street, London SW1P 4NJ); and Jim Cotter's *Prayer in the Day*, a book of mysteries, *Prayer in the Morning*, a book for Day's beginning, *Healing – More or Less*, reflections and prayers in a time of epidemic (from CAIRNS Publications, 185 Topsham Road, Exeter EX2 6AN).
4. *Eucharist and Politics* by Thomas Cullinan OSB (Justice papers published by Catholic Institute for International Relations).

CHAPTER 7

1. See *Liberation Preaching*, Justo and Catherine Gonzalez (Abingdon Press).
2. See John Atherton's *The Scandal of Poverty* (Mowbrays).
3. See *The Prophetic Imagination* and *Hopeful Imagination* both by Walter Brueggeman (Fortress Press).
4. See *Speaking in Parables: A Study in Metaphor and Theology and Metaphorical Theology – Models of God in Religious Language* by Sallie McFague (Fortress Press). Both books have an extensive bibliography on theology as story.

I Believe
Trevor Huddleston

A simple, prayerful series of reflections on the phrases of the Creed. This is a beautiful testament of the strong, quiet inner faith of a man best known for his active role in the Church – and in the world.

The Heart of the Christian Faith
Donald Coggan

The author ". . . presents the essential core of Christianity in a marvellously simple and readable form, quite uncluttered by any excess of theological technicality."
The Yorkshire Post

Be Still and Know
Michael Ramsey

The former Archbishop of Canterbury looks at prayer in the New Testament, at what the early mystics could teach us about it, and at some practical aspects of Christian praying.

Pilgrim's Progress
John Bunyan

"A masterpiece which generation after generation of ordinary men and women have taken to their hearts."
Hugh Ross Williamson

Also available in Fount Paperbacks

BOOKS BY C. S. LEWIS

The Abolition of Man

'It is the most perfectly reasoned defence of Natural Law (Morality) I have ever seen, or believe to exist.'

Walter Hooper

Mere Christianity

'He has a quite unique power for making theology an attractive, exciting and fascinating quest.'

Times Literary Supplement

God in the Dock

'This little book . . . consists of some brilliant pieces . . . This is just the kind of book to place into the hands of an intellectual doubter . . . It has been an unalloyed pleasure to read.'

Marcus Beverley, Christian Herald

The Great Divorce

'Mr Lewis has a rare talent for expressing spiritual truth in fresh and striking imagery and with uncanny acumen . . . it contains many flashes of deep insight and exposures of popular fallacies.'

Church Times

Fount Paperbacks

Fount is one of the leading paperback publishers of religious books and below are some of its recent titles.

- ☐ GETHSEMANE Martin Israel £2.50
- ☐ HIS HEALING TOUCH Michael Buckley £2.50
- ☐ YES TO LIFE David Clarke £2.95
- ☐ THE DIVORCED CATHOLIC Edmund Flood £1.95
- ☐ THE WORLD WALKS BY Sue Masham £2.95
- ☐ C. S. LEWIS: THE MAN AND HIS GOD
  Richard Harries £1.75
- ☐ BEING FRIENDS Peter Levin £2.95
- ☐ DON'T BE AFRAID TO SAY YOU'RE LONELY
  Christopher Martin £2.50
- ☐ BASIL HUME: A PORTRAIT Tony Castle (ed.) £3.50
- ☐ TERRY WAITE: MAN WITH A MISSION
  Trevor Barnes £2.95
- ☐ PRAYING THROUGH PARADOX Charles Elliott £2.50
- ☐ TIMELESS AT HEART C. S. Lewis £2.50
- ☐ THE POLITICS OF PARADISE Frank Field £3.50
- ☐ THE WOUNDED CITY Trevor Barnes £2.50
- ☐ THE SACRAMENT OF THE WORD Donald Coggan £2.95
- ☐ IS THERE ANYONE THERE? Richard MacKenna £1.95

All Fount paperbacks are available through your bookshop or newsagent, or they can be ordered by post from Fount Paperbacks, Cash Sales Department, G.P.O. Box 29, Douglas, Isle of Man. Please send purchase price plus 22p per book, maximum postage £3. Customers outside the UK send purchase price, plus 22p per book. Cheque, postal order or money order. No currency.

NAME (Block letters)_____

ADDRESS _____

_____

_____